LONGMAN IMPRINT BOOKS

Billy Liar

Keith Waterhouse

edited by
Linda Marsh

cover photograph by
Catherine Shakespeare Lane

Longman

Longman Imprint Books
General Editor: Michael Marland CBE MA

Titles in the series
There is a Happy Land Keith Waterhouse
The Human Element Stan Barstow
The Leaping Lad and other stories Sid Chaplin
Conflicting Generations Five television scripts
A Sillitoe Selection *edited by* Michael Marland
***Late Night on Watling Street and other stories** Bill Naughton
Black Boy Richard Wright
Scene Scripts Seven television plays
Ten Western Stories *edited by* C. E. J. Smith
Loves, Hopes, and Fears *edited by* Michael Marland
Cider with Rosie Laurie Lee
Goalkeepers are Crazy Brian Glanville
A James Joyce Selection *edited by* Richard Adams
Out of the Air Five radio plays *edited by* Alfred Bradley
Scene Scripts Two Five television plays
Caribbean Stories *edited by* Michael Marland
An Isherwood Selection *edited by* Geoffrey Halson
A Thomas Hardy Selection *edited by* Geoffrey Halson
The Experience of Parenthood *edited by* Chris Buckton
The Experience of Love *edited by* Michael Marland
Twelve War Stories *edited by* John L. Foster
A Roald Dahl Selection, *edited by* **Roy Blatchford**
A D H Lawrence Selection *edited by* Geoffrey Halson
I'm the King of the Castle Susan Hill
Sliding Leslie Norris
Still Waters Three television plays by Julia Jones
Scene Scripts Three Four television plays *edited by* Roy Blatchford
Television Comedy Scripts Five scripts *edited by* Roy Blatchford
Juliet Bravo Five television scripts
Meetings and Partings Sixteen short stories *compiled by* Michael Marland
Women *compiled and edited by* Maura Healy
Strange Meeting Susan Hill
Looks and Smiles Barry Hines
A Laurie Lee Selection *edited by* Chris Buckton
P'tang, Yang, Kipperbang and other TV plays Jack Rosenthal
Family Circles Five plays *edited by* Alfred Bradley *and* Alison Leake
Humour and Horror Twelve plays *edited by* Caroline Bennitt
Scene Scripts Four Four television plays *edited by* Alison Leake
A Second Roald Dahl Selection *edited by* Helene Fawcett
Scene Scripts Five Four television plays *edited by* Alison Leake
***Race to be Seen** *edited by* Alison Leake and Mark Wheeller
Festival Plays *edited by* Margaret Mackey
Dash and Defiance *edited by* Alison Leake
Hear Me Out *compiled and edited by* Roy Blatchford
A Special Occasion Three plays *edited by* Alison Leake
The Diary of Anne Frank *edited by* Christopher Martin
Wishful Thinking selections from the writings of Keith Waterhouse
Intensive Care Four television plays *edited by* Michael Church
The Woman in Black Susan Hill
John Mortimer Plays Four plays *edited by* Mark Pattenden
Billy Liar Keith Waterhouse

*Cassette available

Contents

Introduction

Had I not spotted in a publisher's catalogue that someone called Alan Sillitoe had a book coming out called *Saturday Night and Sunday Morning*, then *Billy Liar* would have been called *Saturday Night at the Roxy*, and its hero would have been known as Norman Fisher. I wonder how he would have fared then?

Billy has by now been through so many lives – on film, TV, in the theatre both legitimate and musical – that he has long ago taken off on his own, and I can barely remember creating him. But I must have done. I recall only two lucid periods in the life of this novel. The first was when I left ten thousand words of the original draft in a cab – no great loss, since it was in that state awfully pretentious, but it did teach me ever after to attach myself umbilically to my briefcase; and the second was when (I then smoked as I worked) a box of matches exploded in my hand as I wrote the final chapter, and every word of the last few pages had to be painfully tapped out by a blistered, bandaged finger.

But as I say, Billy Liar and I have separate careers these days. He goes his way, I mine. It's nice to bump into him occasionally, but I cannot hold myself responsible for anything he may get up to.

Keith Waterhouse

Chapter One

Lying in bed, I abandoned the facts again and was back in Ambrosia.

By rights, the march-past started in the Avenue of the Presidents, but it was an easy thing to shift the whole thing into Town Square. My friends had vantage seats on the town hall steps where no flag flew more proudly than the tattered blue star of the Ambrosian Federation, the standard we had carried into battle. One by one the regiments marched past, and when they had gone – the Guards, the Parachute Regiment, the King's Own Yorkshire Light Infantry – a hush fell over the crowds and they removed their hats for the proud remnants of the Ambrosian Grand Yeomanry. It was true that we had entered the war late, and some criticised us for that; but out of two thousand who went into battle only seven remained to hear the rebuke. We limped along as we had arrived from the battlefield, the mud still on our shredded uniforms, but with a proud swing to our kilts. The band played 'March of the Movies'. The war memorial was decked with blue poppies, the strange bloom found only in Ambrosia.

I put an end to all this, consciously and deliberately, by going *'Da da da da da da da'* aloud to drive the thinking out of my head. It was a day for big decisions. I recalled how I could always cure myself when I got on one of those counting sprees where it was possible to reach three thousand easily without stopping: I would throw in a confetti of confusing numbers or, if they didn't help, half-remembered quotations and snatches of verse. *'Seventy-three. Nine hundred and six. The Lord is my shepherd, I shall not want, he maketh me to lie down. Four hundred and thirty-five.'*

It was a day for big decisions. I had already determined, more for practical reasons than out of any new policy, to clip the thumb-nail which I have been cultivating until it was a quarter of an inch long. Now, lying under the pale gold eiderdown, staring up at the crinoline ladies craftily fashioned out of silver paper and framed in passe-partout (*they* would be coming down, for a start) I began to abandon the idea of saving the clipping in an ointment box; I would throw it right away, without a backward glance, and from now on, short nails, and a brisk bath each morning. An end, too, to this habit of lying in bed crinkling my toes fifty times for each foot; in future I would be up at seven and an hour's work done before breakfast. There would be no more breath-holding, eye-blinking, nostril-twitching or sucking of the teeth, and this plan would start tomorrow, if not today.

I lay in bed, the toe-crinkling over; now I was stretching the fingers of both hands to their fullest extent, like two star-fish. Sometimes I got an overpowering feeling that my fingers were webbed, like a duck's, and I had to spread them out to block the sensation and prevent it spreading to my feet.

My mother shouted up the stairs: 'Billy? *Bi*lly! *Are* you getting up?' the third call in a fairly well-established series of street cries that graduated from: 'Are you awake, Billy?' to 'It's a quarter past nine, and you can stay in bed all day for all I care,' meaning twenty to nine and time to get up. I waited until she called: 'If I come up there you'll *know* about it' (a variant of number five, usually 'If I come up there I shall *tip* you out') and then I got up.

I put on the old raincoat I used for a dressing-gown, making the resolution that now I must buy a real dressing-gown, possibly a silk one with some kind of dragon motif, and I felt in my pocket for the Player's Weights. I was trying to bring myself up to smoke before breakfast but this time even the idea of it brought on the familiar nausea. I shoved the cigarettes back in my pocket and felt the letter still there, but this time I did not read it. *'He scribbled a few notes on the back of a used envelope.'* The phrase had always appealed to me. I had a pleasing image of a stack of used envelopes, secured by a rubber band, crammed with notes in a thin, spidery handwriting. I took the used envelope out of my pocket with the letter still in it and thought up some jottings. *'Calendars. See S. re job. Write Boon. Thousand??? See Witch re Captain.'* Most of these notes were unnecessary, especially the bit about seeing Witch re Captain; that, along with the calendars, always a part-time worry, and the other bit about seeing S. re job, had kept me awake half the night. As for Thousand???

this was a ghost of idle thinking, the last traces of a plan to write a thousand words each day of a public school story to be entitled *The Two Schools at Gripminster*. Having conceived the plan in early August, I was already thirty-four thousand words behind on the schedule. There were long periods of time when my own ambition was to suck a Polo mint right through without it breaking in my mouth; others when I would retreat into Ambrosia and sketch out the new artists' settlement on route eleven, and they would be doing profiles of me on television, 'Genius – or Madman?'

I put the ballpoint away and shoved the envelope back in my pocket, and on the cue of cry number seven, by far my favourite ('Your boiled egg's stone cold and *I'm* not cooking another'), I went downstairs.

Hillcrest, as the house was called (although not by me) was the kind of dwelling where all the windows are leaded in a fussy criss-cross, except one, which is a porthole. Our porthole was at the turn of the stairs and here I paused to rub the heel of my slipper against the stair-rod, another habit I would be getting out of henceforth. Shuffling there, I could see out across the gravel to the pitch-painted garage with its wordy, gold-painted sign: 'Geo. Fisher & Son, Haulage Contractors, Distance No Object. "The Moving Firm" Tel: 2573. Stamp, Signs.' The sign was inaccurate. I was the son referred to, but in fact the old man had gone to great trouble to keep me out of the family business, distance no object. What really got on my nerves, however, was the legend 'Stamp, Signs' which was almost as big as the advertisement itself. Eric Stamp had been the white-haired boy of the art class when we were at Stradhoughton Technical together, and was now my colleague at Shadrack and Duxbury's. It was his ambition to set up in the sign-writing business full-time, and I for one was not stopping him.

Anyway, the fact that the garage doors were not open yet meant that the old man was still at home and there were going to be words exchanged about last night's outing. I slopped down into the hall, took the *Stradhoughton Echo* out of the letter-box, where it would have remained all day if the rest of the family had anything to do with it, and went into the lounge. It was a day for big decisions.

The breakfast ceremony at Hillcrest had never been my idea of fun. I had made one disastrous attempt to break the monotony of it, entering the room one day with my eyes shut and my arms outstretched like a sleep-walker, announcing in a shaky, echo-chamber voice: 'Ay York-shire breakfast scene. Ay polished table, one leaf out, covahed diagonally by ay white tablecloth, damask, with grrreen strip bordah. Sauce-stain to the right, blackberry stain to the centre. Kellogg's cornflakes, Pyrex dishes, plate of fried bread. Around the table, the following personnel: fathah, mothah, grandmothah, one vacant place.' None of this had gone down well. I entered discreetly now, almost shiftily, taking in with a dull eye the old man's pint mug disfigured by a crack that was no longer mistaken for a hair, and the radio warming up for Yesterday in Parliament. It was a choice example of the hygienic family circle, but to me it had taken on the glazed familiarity of some old print such as When Did You Last See Your Father? I was greeted by the usual breathing noises.

'You decided to get up, then,' my mother said, slipping easily into the second series of conversations of the day. My stock replies were 'Yes,' 'No, I'm still in bed' and a snarled 'What does it look like?' according to mood. Today I chose 'Yes' and sat down to my boiled egg, stone cold as threatened. This made it a quarter to nine.

The old man looked up from some invoices and said: 'And you can start getting bloody well dressed before you come down in a morning.' So far the dialogue was taking a fairly conventional route and I was tempted to throw in one of the old stand-bys, 'Why do you always begin your sentences with an "And"?' Gran, another dress fanatic who always seemed to be fully and even elaborately attired even at two in the morning when she slunk downstairs after the soda-water, chipped in: 'He wants to burn that raincoat, then he'll have to get dressed of a morning.' One of Gran's peculiarities, and she had many, was that she would never address anyone directly but always went through an intermediary, if necessary some static object such as a cupboard. Doing the usual decoding I gathered that she was addressing my mother and that he who should burn the raincoat was the old man, and he who would have to get dressed of a morning was me. 'I gather,' I began, 'that he who should burn the raincoat —— ' but the old man interrupted:

'And what bloody time did you get in *last* night? If you can call it last night. This bloody morning, more like.'

I sliced the top off my boiled egg, which in a centre favouring tapping the top with a spoon and peeling the bits off was always calculated to annoy, and said lightly: '*I* don't know. 'Bout half-past eleven, quarter to twelve.'

The old man said: 'More like one o'clock, with your half-past bloody eleven! Well you can bloody well and start coming in of a night-time. I'm not having *you* gallivanting round at all hours, not at your bloody age.'

'Who *are* you having gallivanting round, then?' I asked, the wit rising for the day like a pale and watery sun.

My mother took over, assuming the clipped, metallic voice of the morning interrogation. '*What were you doing down Foley Bottoms at nine o'clock last night?*'

I said belligerently: 'Who says I was down at Foley Bottoms?'

'Never mind who says, or who doesn't say. You *were* there, and it wasn't that Barbara you were with, neither.'

'He wants to make up his mind who he *is* going with,' Gran said.

There was a rich field of speculation for me here. Since my mother had never even met the Witch – the one to whom she referred by her given name of Barbara – or Rita either – the one involved in the Foley Bottoms episode, that is – I wondered how she managed to get her hands on so many facts without actually hiring detectives.

I said: 'Well you want to tell whoever saw me to mind their own fizzing business.'

'It *is* our business,' my mother said. 'And don't you be so cheeky!' I pondered over the absent friend who had supplied the Foley Bottoms bulletin. Mrs Olmonroyd? Ma Walker? Stamp? *The Witch herself?* I had a sudden, hideous notion that the Witch was in league with my mother and that they were to spring some dreadful coup upon me the following day when, with a baptism of lettuce and pineapple chunks, the Witch was due to be introduced to the family at Sunday tea.

Gran said: 'If she's coming for her tea tomorrow she wants to tell her. If she doesn't, I will.' My mother interpreted this fairly intelligently and said: 'I'm *going* to tell her, don't you fret yourself.' She slid off down a chuntering landslide of recrimination until the old man, reverting to the main theme, came back with the heavy artillery.

'He's not bloody well old enough to stay out half the night,

I've told him before. He can start coming in of a night, or else go and live somewhere else.'

This brought me beautifully to what I intended to be the text for the day, but now that the moment had come I felt curiously shy and even a little sick at the idea of my big decisions. I allowed my mother to pour me a grudging cup of tea. I picked up the sugar with the tongs so as to fall in with house rules. I fingered the used envelope in my raincoat pocket, see S. re job. I cleared my throat and felt again the urge to yawn that had been with me like a disease for as long as I could remember, and that for all I knew *was* a disease and a deadly one at that. The need to yawn took over from all the other considerations and I began to make the familiar Channel-swimmer mouthings, fishing for the ball of air at the back of my throat. The family returned to rummage among their breakfast plates and, aware that the moment had gone by, I said:

'I've been *off*ered that job in London.'

The replies were predictable, so predictable that I had already written them down, although not on a used envelope, and had meant to present the family with this wryly-humorous summing-up of their little ways as some kind of tolerant benediction on them after they spoke, which according to my notes was as follows:

Old man: 'What bloody job?'

Mother: 'How do you mean, you've been offered it?'

Gran: 'What's he talking about, I thought he was going to be a cartooner, last I heard.'

Another of Gran's whimsicalities was that she could not, or more likely would not, remember the noun for the person who draws cartoons. She threw me a baleful glare and I decided not to bring out the predictions but to carry on as I had planned the night before or, as the old man would have it, the early hours of the morning, tossing and turning under the pale gold eiderdown.

'That job with Danny Boon. When I wrote to him,' I said.

I had often likened the conversation at Hillcrest to the route of the old No. 14 tram. Even when completely new subjects were being discussed, the talk rattled on along the familiar track, stopping to load on festering arguments from the past, and culminating at the terminus of the old man's wrath.

'What job with Danny Boon?' This line – together with a rhubarb-rhubarb chorus of 'What's he talking about, Danny Boon?' – was optional for the whole family, but was in fact spoken by my mother.

'The job I was *telling* you about.'

'What job, you've never told *me* about no job.'

It was obviously going to be one of the uphill treks. The whole family knew well enough about my ambition, or one of my ambitions, to write scripts for comedy. They knew how Danny Boon, who was not so famous then as he is now, had played a week at the Stradhoughton Empire. They knew, because I had told them four times, that I had taken him some material – including my 'thick as lead' catchline which Boon now uses all the time – and how he had liked it. ('Well how do you know he'll pay you anything?' my mother had said.) They knew I had asked him for a *job*. Thank God, I thought, as I pushed my boiled egg aside with the yolk gone and the white untouched, that they don't ask me who Danny Boon is when he's at home.

'Why does he always leave the white of his egg?' asked Gran. 'It's all goodness, just thrown down the sink.'

The remark was so completely irrelevant that even my mother, always a willing explorer down the back-doubles on the conversational map, ignored it. Shouts of 'What about your job at Shadrack and *Dux*bury's?' and 'Who do you think's going to *keep* you?' began to trickle through but I maintained my hysterical calm, wearing my sensitivity like armour. Above everything I could hear the querulous tones of Gran, going over and over again: 'What's he on about? What's he on about? What's he on about? What's he on about?'

I took a deep breath and made it obvious that I was taking a deep breath, and said: 'Look, there is a comedian. The comedian's name is Danny Boon. B- double O-N. He does not write his own scripts. He gets other people to do it for him. He likes my material. He thinks he can give me regular work.'

My mother said: 'How do you mean, he likes your material?'

I brought out the heavy sigh and the clenched teeth. 'Look. This pepper-pot is Danny Boon. This salt-cellar is my material. Danny Boon is looking for material —— ' I turned the blue plastic pepper-pot on them like a ray-gun. 'He sees my flaming material. So he flaming well asks for it.'

''Ere, rear, rear, watch your bloody language! With your flaming this and flaming that! At meal-times! You're not in bloody London yet, you know!'

'He's gone too far,' said Gran, complacently.

I went: 'Sssssss!' through my teeth. 'For crying out loud!' I slipped back a couple of notches into the family dialect and said: 'Look, do you wanna know or don't you? Cos if you do ah'll tell you, and if you don't ah won't.'

They sat with pursed lips, my mother heaving at the bosom and the old man scowling over his bills and the Woodbine ash filling up his eggshell. The radio took over the silence and filled it for a moment with some droning voice.

'Try *again*,' I said. I took another deep breath, which developed into a yawning fit.

'You just eat your breakfast, and don't have so much off,' my mother said. 'Else get your mucky self washed. And stop always yawning at meal-times. You don't get enough sleep, that's all that's wrong with you.'

'And get to bloody work,' the old man said.

I pushed back the polished chair, about whose machine-turned legs I had once had so much to say, and went into the kitchen. It was five minutes past nine. I leaned against the sink in an angry torpor, bombing and blasting each one of them to hell. I lit a stealthy Player's Weight, and thought of the steel-bright autumn day in front of me, and began to feel better. I breathed heavily again, this time slowly and luxuriously, and began to grope through the coils of fuse-wire in the kitchen drawer for the old man's electric razor. I switched on, waited for a tense second for the bellowed order from the lounge to put the thing away and buy one of my own, and then began my thinking.

I was spending a good part of my time, more of it as each day passed, on this thinking business. Sometimes I could squander the whole morning on it, and very often the whole evening and a fair slice of the night hours too. I had two kinds of thinking (three, if ordinary thoughts were counted) and I had names for them, applied first jocularly and then mechanically. I called them No. 1 thinking and No. 2 thinking. No. 1 thinking was voluntary, but No. 2 thinking was not; it concerned itself with obsessional speculations about the scope and nature of disease (such as a persistent yawn that was probably symptomatic of sarcoma of the jaw), the probable consequences of actual misdemeanours, and the solutions to desperate problems, such as what would one do, what would one actually *do*, in the case of having a firework jammed in one's ear by mischievous boys. The way out of all this was to lull myself into a No. 1 thinking bout, taking the fast excursion to Ambrosia, including in hypothetical conversations with Bertrand Russell, fusing and magnifying the ordinary thoughts of the day so that I was a famous comedian at the Ambrosia State Opera, the only stage personality ever to reach the rank of president.

Propped up against the gas-stove, buzzing away with the old man's razor, I began to do some No. 1 thinking on the subject of the family. This usually took a reasonably noble form: riding home to Hillcrest loaded with money, putting the old man on his feet, forgiving and being forgiven. My mother would be put into furs, would feel uneasy in them at first, but would be touched and never lose her homely ways. Grandma married Councillor Duxbury and the pair of them, apple-cheeked, lived in a thatched cottage high up in the dales, out of sight. That was the usual thing. But this morning, in harder mood, I began to plan entirely new parents for myself. They were of the modern, London, kind. They had allowed, in fact *encouraged*, me to smoke from the age of thirteen (Marcovitch) and when I came home drunk my No. 1 mother would look up from her solitaire and groan: 'Oh God, how dreary! Billy's drunk again!' I announced at breakfast that I was going to start out on my own. My No. 1 father – the old man disguised as a company director – clapped me on the back and said: '*And* about time, you old loafer. Simone and I were thinking of kicking you out of the old nest any day now. Better come into the library and talk about the money end.' As for Gran, she didn't exist.

The thinking and the shaving finished concurrently. I switched off and began brooding over the matter of the black bristles under my chin which, shave as I might, would never come smooth. I dropped back into my torpor, a kind of vacuum annexe to the No. 2 thinking, and began scraping the back of my hand against the bristles, listening to the noise of it and wondering whether there was something wrong with me. The old man came through into the kitchen, putting on his jacket on his way to the garage.

'And you can buy your own bloody razor and stop using mine,' he said without stopping. I called: *'Eighty-four!'* supposedly the number of times he had used the word 'bloody' that morning, a standing joke (at least with me), but he had gone out. The business of going to London was shelved, forgotten or, as I suspected, completely uncomprehended.

I went through the lounge and upstairs. My mother, as I passed her, chanted automatically: 'You'll-set-off-one-of-these-days-and-meet-yourself-coming-back,' one of a series of remarks tailored, I liked to fancy, to fit the exact time taken by me from kitchen door to hall door. There had been a time when I had tried to get the family to call these stock sayings of hers 'Motherisms'. Nobody ever knew what I was talking about.

Swilling myself in the bathroom I found the business of the bristles on my chin leading, as I had known it would, into a definite spasm of No. 2 thinking. I wondered first if I were developing ingrowing hair, like those people whose throats tickle every six weeks and who have to go into hospital to get it removed, and then I ran through the usual repertoire, polio, cancer, T.B. and a new disease, unique in medical history, called Fisher's Yawn. Nowadays these attacks, occurring more or less whenever I had a spare minute, usually culminated at the point where I began to wonder what would happen if I were taken to hospital, died even, and they found out about the calendars.

My mother shouted up the stairs: 'You'll never get into *town* at this rate, never mind London! It's after half-past nine!' but by now the calendar theme had me in its grip, and I staggered into my bedroom, gasping and clawing for breath, doing some deep-level No. 2 thinking on the subject.

It was now September. The calendars had been given to me to post about two weeks before Christmas of the previous year. This meant that this particular problem had been on the agenda for over nine months or, as I sometimes worked it out, six thousand five hundred and twenty-eight hours. The calendars were stiff cardboard efforts measuring ten inches by eight, each bearing a picture of a cat looking at a dog, the legend 'Rivals' and, overprinted in smudgy olive type, 'Shadrack and Duxbury, Funeral Furnishers. Taste' – then a little star – 'Tact' – and another little star – 'Economy.' They were prestige jobs for Shadrack's contacts, people like the directors of the crematorium and parsons who might ring up with a few tip-offs, and for good customers like the Alderman Burrows Old People's Home, with whom Shadrack and Duxbury's had a standing account. I had omitted to post them in order to get at the postage money, which I had kept for myself. I had hidden the calendars in the stockroom in the office basement for a while and then, tired of the hideous reel of No. 2 thinking where Shadrack lifted the coffin lid and found them, had gradually transferred them home. A few I had already destroyed, taking them out of the house one by one at night and tearing them to shreds, dropping them in a paper-chase over Stradhoughton Moor and sweating over an image of the police picking them up and piecing them together. I had got rid of fourteen in this way. The rest were in a tin trunk under my bed. There were two hundred and eleven of them.

I dressed, making another mental note to look up *Every Man's Own Lawyer* and find out the penalties for this particular crime. 'Pay attention to me, Fisher. I have thought very carefully about sending you to prison. Only your youth and the fact that your employers have spoken so highly of your abilities . . .' Tying my tie, I began to imagine myself in Armley Jail, impressing the governor with my intelligence, making friends with the padre; and for a short while I was back on the No. 1 thinking, a luxury I could ill afford at half-past nine on a working morning.

'Billy! If you're not out of this house in five minutes I shall push you out!'

I put on my jacket and pulled the old japanned trunk from under the bed. The piece of stamp edging was still in position across the lid. A long while ago, when it had contained no more than the scribbled postcards from Liz and a few saccharine notes from the Witch, I had started to call this trunk my Guilt Chest. Any grain of facetiousness there had been in this description had long since disappeared.

I lifted the lid gingerly, jolted and disturbed as usual by the vast number of calendars there seemed to be, stacked dozens deep in their thick brown envelopes, addressed in my own broad handwriting to Dr H. Rich, P. W. Horniman,

Esq., J.P., the Rev. D. L. P. Tack, the Warden, Stradhoughton Workpeople's Hostel. Beside the calendars, nestling in their own dark hollow of the Guilt Chest, were the love letters, the bills the old man had given me to post, the aphrodisiac tablets that Stamp had got for me, the cellophaned, leggy copy of Ritzy Stories, and the letter my mother had once written to Housewives' Choice. I could picture her sitting down with the Stephens' ink bottle and the Basildon Bond, and I could never explain to myself why I had not posted the letter or why I had opened it under cover of the Guilt Chest lid. *'Dear Sir, Just a few lines to let you know how much I enjoy Housewife's "Choice" every day, I always listen no matter what I am doing, could you play (Just a Song at Twilight) for me though I don't suppose you get time to play everyone that writes to you, but this is my "favourite song." You see my husband often used to sing it when we a bit younger than we are now, I will quite understand if you cannot play. Yours respectfully (Mrs) N. Fisher. PS. My son also write songs, but I suppose there is not much chance for him as he has not had the training. We are just ordinary folk.'* The debates I had had with my mother on the ordinary folk motif, in long and eloquent streams of No. 1 thinking, would have filled Housewives' Choice ten times over.

Snapped together by a rubber band, like the used envelopes I had fancied for myself, was the thin pack of postcards that Liz had written to me on her last expedition but one. They were matter-of-fact little notes, full of tediously interesting details about the things she had seen in Leicester, Welwyn Garden City and the other places where whatever urge possessing her had taken her; but at least they were literate. I felt mildly peculiar to be treasuring love letters for their grammar, but there was nothing else I could treasure them for. Sometimes I could think about Liz, think properly on the ordinary plane, for a full minute, before we were both whisked off into Ambrosia, myself facing trial for sedition and she a kind of white-faced Eva Peron in the crowd.

I took one of the calendars out of the Guilt Chest and stuffed it under my pullover. If I was going to London in a week it meant that I had one hundred and sixty-eight hours to dispose of two hundred and eleven calendars. Say, for safety, two calendars an hour between now and next Saturday. I took out another three and crammed them half under my pullover and half under the top of my trousers.

Rummaging in the Guilt Chest, I spotted the flat white packet of supposed aphrodisiacs, the 'passion pills' as Stamp, shoving them grubbily into my hand in a fit of remorse, fear and generosity, had called them. I put Liz out of my mind and began thinking about Rita and then, making a definite decision, about the Witch. I put the passion pills in my side pocket and bent to close the Guilt Chest, the calendars stiff under my ribs and the sharp corners showing through the cable-weave of my pullover. I replaced the stamp edging, four inches from the handle on the right-hand side, pushed the trunk carefully under the bed and went downstairs, feeling like a walking Guilt Chest myself. In the hall I put on my outdoor raincoat and buttoned it to the waist before going into the lounge.

'He'll be *buried* in a raincoat,' said Gran, almost, in fact completely, automatically. She was rubbing viciously at the sideboard with a check duster, a daily gruelling which she imagined paid for her keep. It was to the sideboard that she addressed herself, because my mother was in the kitchen.

It was long past any time at all for a working morning. The last late typists, their bucket bags stuffed with deodorants and paper handkerchiefs, had clacked past on their way to the bus shelter. A morning hush had settled over the house. There were specks of dust in the sunlight and the stiff smell of Mansion Polish. The radio emphasised the lateness with an unfamiliar voice, talking about some place where they had strange customs; it was like going long past one's station on the last train.

I called: 'I'm off, mother!'

'Well don't hurrv yourself, will you?' she called back, following her voice into the lounge. I paused with my hand running up and down the brown bakelite finger-plate on the door.

'Might as well give my notice in today, if I'm going to London,' I said. My mother pressed her lips together in a thin purple line and began bundling up the tablecloth, taking it by the corners to keep the crumbs in.

'You want to make up your mind what you *do* want to do!' she said primly.

'I *know* what I'm going to do. I'm going to work for Danny Boon.'

'Well how do you know, you've never done that sort of

thing before. You can't switch and change and swop about just when you feel like it. You've got your living to earn now, you know!'

She was trying to talk kindly, making a real effort at it but drawing the effort back, like someone whispering across a bridge. I was touched, fleetingly. I said, trying hard myself: 'Any road, we'll talk about it later,' a gruff and oblique statement of affection that, I could see, was received and understood.

I left the house, ignoring the old man who was messing about with the lorry in the road outside. If I can walk all the way down Cherry Row without blinking my eyelids, I told myself, it will be all all right. I kept my eyes wide and burning long past Greenman's sweet-shop, past the clay cavities where the semis were not built yet; then Mrs Olmonroyd came past, spying. I clapped my eyes shut and wished her a civil good morning. I felt the calendars under my jacket and wondered why I had brought them out and what I was going to do with them, and what I was going to do about everything.

Chapter Two

'The very name of Stradhoughton,' Man o' the Dales had written in the *Stradhoughton Echo* one morning when there was nothing much doing, 'conjures up sturdy buildings of honest native stone, gleaming cobbled streets, and that brackish air which gives this corner of Yorkshire its own especial *piquancy*.' Man o' the Dales put piquancy in italics, not me.

My No. 1 thinking often featured long sessions with Man o' the Dales in whatever pub the boys on the *Echo* used, and there I would put him right on his facts. The cobbled streets, gleaming or otherwise, had long ago been ripped up with the tramlines and re-lined with concrete slabs or tarmacadam – gleaming tarmacadam I would *grant* him, stabbing him in the chest with the stocky briar which in this particular role I affected. The brackish air I was no authority on, except to say that when the wind was in a certain direction it smelled of burning paint. As for the honest native stone, our main street, Moorgate, was – despite the lying reminiscences of old men like Councillor Duxbury who remembered sheep-troughs where the X-L Disc Bar now stands – exactly like any other High Street in Great Britain. Woolworth's looked like Woolworth's, the Odeon looked like the Odeon, and the *Stradhoughton Echo's* own office, which Man o' the Dales must have seen, looked like a public lavatory in honest native white tile. I had a fairly passionate set piece all worked out on the subject of rugged Yorkshire towns, with their rugged neon signs and their rugged plate-glass and plastic shop-fronts, but so far nobody had given me the opportunity to start up on the theme.

'Dark satanic mills I can put up with,' I would say, pushing my tobacco pouch along the bar counter. 'They're part of the picture. But' – puff, puff – 'when it comes to dark satanic power stations, dark satanic housing estates, and dark satanic teashops —— '

'That's the trouble with you youngsters,' said Man o' the

Dales, propping his leather-patched elbows on the seasoned bar. 'You want progress, but you want all the Yorkshire tradition as well. You can't have both.'

'I want progress,' I retorted, making with the briar. 'But I want a Yorkshire tradition of progress.'

'That's good. Can I use that?' said Man o' the Dales.

Anyway, satanic or not, it was the usual Saturday morning down in town, the fat women rolling along on their bad feet like toy clowns in pudding basins, the grey-faced men reviewing the sporting pinks. Along Market Street, where the new glass-fronted shops spilled out their sagging lengths of plywood and linoleum, there were still the old-fashioned stalls, lining the gutter with small rotten apples and purple tissue paper. The men shouted: 'Do I ask fifteen bob, do I ask twelve and a tanner? I do *not*. I do not ask you for ten bob. I do not ask you for three half crowns. Gimme five bob, five bob, five bob, five bob, five bob.' Frowning women, their black, scratched handbags crammed with half-digested grievances, pushed through the vegetable stalls to the steps of the rates office.

Off Market Street there was a little alley called St Botolph's Passage, the centre of most of Stradhoughton's ready-money betting. Besides the bookies' shops, the stinking urinal, the sly chemist's with red rubber gloves and big sex books in the window, and the obscure one-man businesses mooning behind the dark doorways, there was a pub, a dyer's and cleaner's, and Shadrack and Duxbury's, tasteful funerals. Many were the jokes about St Botolph and his passage, but even more were those about the dyers and the undertakers.

The exterior of Shadrack's, where I now paused to take my traditional deep breath before entering, showed a conflict of personalities between young Shadrack and old Duxbury, the two partners. Young Shadrack, taking advantage of Duxbury's only trip abroad, a reciprocal visit by the town council to Lyons (described by Man o' the Dales as the Stradhoughton of France), had pulled out the Dickensian windows, bottle-glass and all, and substituted modern plate-glass and a shop sign of raised stainless steel lettering. Thus another piece of old Stradhoughton bit the dust and the new effect was of a chip shop on a suburban housing estate. Councillor Duxbury had returned only just in time to salve the old window-dressing from the wreckage, and this remained: a smudgy sign by Stamp reading 'Tasteful Funeral's, "Night or Day Service"' (which, as my other colleague Arthur had said, needed only an exclamation mark in brackets to complete it) and a piece of purple cloth on which there was deposited a white vase, the shape of a lead weight, inscribed to the memory of a certain Josiah Olroyd. The reason Josiah Olroyd's vase was in Shadrack's window and not in the corporation cemetery was that his name had been misspelled, and the family had not unreasonably refused to accept goods ordered. The Olroyd vase always served to remind me of a ghastly error with some coffin nameplates in which I had been involved, a business that was far from finished yet, and it was with this thought uppermost in a fairly crowded mind that, ninety minutes late, I entered Shadrack and Duxbury's.

The shop bell rang and, behaving exactly like a Pavlov dog, Stamp got up and began, elaborately, to put on his coat.

'Must be going-home time, Fisher's come,' he said.

I ignored him and addressed Arthur.

'Is he in?' I jerked my head towards Shadrack's door.

'Just come in this minute,' said Arthur. 'You can say you were in the bog.'

I hissed with relief and flopped down at my desk, between Stamp and Arthur. Every day, sitting tensed at the front of the bus, pushing it with my hands to make it faster, I had this race to the office with Shadrack. Duxbury didn't matter; he never came rolling in until eleven and in any case he was so old that he could never remember who worked for him. It was Shadrack, with his little notebooks, and the propelling pencil rattling against his teeth, who gave all the trouble. 'It's been noticed that you were half an hour late again this morning.' He always said 'It's been noticed.' 'It's been noticed that you haven't sent those accounts off yet.'

'I'm off to tell him what time you came in,' sniggered Stamp, and I was obliged to murmur 'You do,' the passing acknowledgement of his feeble jest. Stamp called himself a 'clurk' and did not go very much beyond jokes of the Mary-Rose-sat-on-a-pin-Mary-Rose variety. He now started on his morning performance.

'Hey, that tart on telly last night! Where she bent forward over that piano! *Coarrrr!*'

It was the first duty of Arthur and myself to nip this quietly in the bud.

'What make?' said Arthur innocently.

'What make what?'

'What make was the piano?'

Stamp sneered: 'Oh, har har. Some say good old Arthur.'

We got down to our work, what there was of it. Shadrack and Duxbury's was dull and comfortable as offices go. It was done throughout in sleepy chocolate woodwork, which Shadrack, dreaming of pinewood desks and Finnish wallpapers, had not yet got his hands on. Our task was to do the letters, make up the funeral accounts, run the errands and greet prospective customers with a suitably gloomy expression before shuffling them off on to Shadrack. September was a quiet month and Saturday was a quiet morning; we all had our own pursuits to work on. Stamp, head on one side, tongue cocked out of the corner of his mouth, spent most of his time making inky posters for the youth club *'Have you paid your "subs"? If not, "why not"!!!'* Arthur and I would sit around trying to write songs together, or sometimes I would tinker with *The Two Schools at Gripminster.*

'You couldn't see what make it was, she was bending too far over it,' Stamp said at last. I did not look at him, but I knew that he was describing a bosom with his hands.

'Penny's dropped,' Arthur said.

'Penny-farthing more like,' I said. 'It's been earning interest while he thought that one up.'

'Write that one down,' Arthur said.

'Joke over,' said Stamp.

There was nothing in the in-tray. I got *The Two Schools at Gripminster* out of my desk drawer and stared vacantly at what I had written of my thirty-four thousand words. *'"I say, weed! Aren't you a new bug?" Sammy Brown turned to greet the tall, freckle-faced boy who walked across the quad towards him. Sammy's second name was appropriate – for the face of this sturdy young fellow was as brown as a berry. W. Fisher. William Fisher. The Two Schools at Gripminster, by William Fisher. William L. Fisher. W. L. Fisher. Two-School Sammy, by W. L. P. Fisher. Two Schools at Gripminster: A Sammy Brown Story by W. L. P. Fisher. The Sammy Brown Omnibus. W. Lashwood Fisher. W. de L. Fisher.'* I looked at it for some time, thought *'William Fisher: His Life and Times'* but did not write it down, then put the paper back in the drawer. The four chunky calendars under my pullover hurt my chest when I leaned forward over the desk. I began thinking of Danny Boon and the letter I had better write to him, and about Shadrack and the letter I had better write to *him*.

'I've got something unpleasant to say to our Mr Shadrack this morning,' I said to Arthur.

'You've got something unpleasant to say to our Mr Shadrack this morning?' repeated Arthur, dropping into the Mr Bones and Mr Jones routine in which we conducted most of our exchanges. I decided not to tell Arthur just yet about the London business but to while half an hour away in the usual manner. 'Anything I say to Mr Shadrack would be unpleasant,' I said.

'Kindly leave the undertaker's,' Arthur said.

'Tell me, Mr Crabtree, what are the Poles doing in Russia?'

'I don't know, Mr Fisher, what are the Poles doing in Russia?'

'Holding up the telegraph wires, same as everywhere else.'

'That's not what these ladies and gentlemen have come to hear.'

I jumped to my feet, clutching the ruler from my desk. 'Have a care, Mr Crabtree! If I fire this rod it'll be curtains for you!'

'Why so, Mr Fisher?'

'It's a curtain rod.'

'I don't wish to know that.'

Stamp plodded in: 'Same here, it's got whiskers on it, that one.' We had explained to him fifty times over that that was the whole bloody *point*, but the idea would not sink in. It always led Stamp to his own jokes.

'If a barber shaves a barber, who talks?'

Arthur and I, deadpan, said: 'Who?'

'Joke over,' Stamp said, weakly. He went back to the poster he was doing for a pea-and-pie supper out Treadmill way. Arthur started typing out the new song we had written. I got going on the letter.

Dear Mr Boon,

Many thanks for your letter of September 2 ——

Dear Mr Boon,

Yes! I should be delighted to come to London ——

Dear Mr Boon,
I will be in London next Saturday ——

The idea of being in London next Saturday, put down on paper and staring me in the face, filled my bowels with quick-flushing terror. For as long as I could remember, I had been enjoying rich slabs of No. 1 thinking about London, coughing my way through the fog to the Odd Man Out Club, Chelsea, with its chess tables and friendly, intelligent girls. I was joint editor, with the smiling 'Jock' Osonolu, a Nigerian student, of the club's sensational wall-sheet, modelled somewhat on the lines of the Ambrosia *Times-Advocate*. I would live in a studio high over the Embankment, sometimes with a girl called Ann, a Londoner herself and as vivacious as they come, but more often with Liz, not Liz as she actually existed but touched up with a No. 1 ponytail to become my collaborator on a play for theatre in the round. Sometimes I could see myself starving on the Embankment, the tramp-poet; and now, sitting at my desk, the idea of *actually* starving on the Embankment suddenly presented itself to me. I switched over into the No. 2 thinking with a grinding of the points inside my stomach and there I was, feeling for the actual pangs of hunger and counting the hot pennies in my pocket. Five shillings left, one egg and chips leaves three and nine, doss down at Rowton House, two and nine. Evening paper twopence-halfpenny, breakfast a tanner, call it two bob, two bob, two bob. I do not ask for ten bob, ladies, I do not ask you for three half crowns. Gimme two bob, two bob, two bob, and back I was on the No. 1, the poet stallholder of Petticoat Lane.

The door-bell tinkled and we put on our funeral faces but it was nobody, only Councillor Duxbury. He crossed the floor to his own office with an old man's shuffle, putting all his thought into the grip of his stick and the pattern of the faded, broken lino. A thick, good coat sat heavily on his bowed back, and there were enamelled medallions on his watch-chain. At the door of his room he half-turned, moving his whole body like an old robot, and muttered: 'Morning, lads.'

We chanted, half-dutifully, half-ironically: 'Good morning, Councillor Duxbury,' and directly the door was closed, began our imitation of him. 'It's *Coun*cillor Duxbury, lad, *Coun*cillor Duxbury. Tha wun't call Lord Harewood mister, would tha? *Coun*cillor, that's mah title. Now think on.'

'Ah'm just about thraiped,' said Arthur in broad dialect. The word was one we had made up to use in the Yorkshire dialect routine, where we took the Michael out of Councillor Duxbury and people like him. Duxbury prided himself on his dialect which was practically unintelligible even to seasoned Yorkshiremen.

'Tha's getten more bracken ivvery day, lad,' I said.

'Aye, an' fair scritten anall,' said Arthur.

'Tha mun laik wi' t' gangling-iron.'

'Aye.'

We swung into the other half of the routine, which was Councillor Duxbury remembering, as he did every birthday in an interview with the *Stradhoughton Echo*. Arthur screwed up his face into the lined old man's wrinkles and said:

'Course, all this were fields when I were a lad.'

' – and course, ah'd nobbut one clog to mah feet when ah come to Stradhoughton,' I said in the wheezing voice.

'Tha could get a meat pie and change out o' fourpence ——'

'Aye, an' a box at t' Empire and a cab home at t' end on it.'

'Ah had to tak' a cab home because ah only had one clog', said Arthur.

'Oh, I'll *use* that,' I said, resuming my normal voice. *'Bastard.'*

'Bar-steward,' said Stamp, automatically.

Every Saturday night I did a club turn down at one of the pubs in Clogiron Lane, near where we lived. It was a comedy act, but not the kind of thing Danny Boon would be interested in: a slow-burning, Yorkshire monologue that was drummed up mainly by Arthur and me at these sessions in the office. Arthur was more interested in the singing side. He did a turn with the band at the Roxy twice a week, Wednesdays and Saturdays, trying vainly to get them to play the songs we had written between us. When my own turn was finished I would hurry over to the Roxy to listen to him, pretending that I was whisking from one theatre to another to catch a promising act that I was thinking of booking.

As for Stamp, he did nothing at all except loll about in the Roxy, waving his arms about and mouthing 'Woodchopper's Ball' when the band played it.

'Saw that bint you used to knock about with 's morning,' he said, when the Duxbury routine was over.

'You what?'

'That bint. Her that always used to be ringing you up.'

I ran flippantly back through the sequence of disasters, Audrey, Peggy, Lil, that bint from Morecambe. A depression grew inside me as I traced them back almost to my school-days. When I recognised the depression, I knew whom he was talking about.

I said lightly, knowing what was coming: '*What* bint, for Christ sake?'

'That scruffy-looking one. Her that always wore that suède coat.'

I poured unconcern into my voice. 'Who – Liz What's-her-name?'

'Yer, Woodbine Lizzy. Randy as a rattlesnake, isn't she? She hasn't got a new coat yet.'

So Liz was back in town. I liked the phrase 'back in town', as though she had just ridden in on a horse, and I toyed with it for a second, so as not to think about her. Drive you out of town. City limits. Get out of town, Logan, I'm warning you for the last time.

It was a month ago since she had left last, with only a chance good-bye, and this time there had been no postcards. It was part of the nature of Liz to disappear from time to time and I was proud of her bohemianism, crediting her with a soul-deep need to get away and straighten out her personality, or to find herself, or something; but in less romantic moments I would fall to wondering whether she was tarting round the streets with some American airman. I had no real feeling for her, but there was always some kind of pain when she went away, and when the pain yielded nothing, I converted it, like an alchemist busy with the seaweed, into something approaching love.

'Where did you see her?' I asked.

'*I* don't know. Walking up Infirmary Street,' said Stamp. 'Why, frightened she's got another boy friend?' he said in his nauseating, elbow-prodding way.

I said carefully: 'Thought she'd gone to Canada or somewhere,' naming the first country that came into my head.

'What's she come back for, then?' said Stamp.

I was trying to find a cautious way of going on with it when Arthur came to the rescue. He had been handling the switchboard.

'Never use a preposition to end a sentence with,' he said.

I often told myself that I had no friends, only allies, banded together in some kind of conspiracy against the others. Arthur was one of them. We spoke together mainly in catchphrases, hidden words that the others could not understand.

'I might ask you to not split infinitives,' I said gratefully, in the light relieved voice.

'Hear about the bloke who shot the owl?' said Arthur. 'It kept saying to who instead of to whom.'

'Shouldn't it be Who's Whom instead of Who's Who?' I said, not for the first time that week. Even our ordinary conversations were like the soft-shoe shuffle routine with which we enlivened the ordinary day. I was perfectly aware that I was stalling, and I turned back to Stamp.

'Did you speak to her?'

'Speak to who?'

'To whom. Woodbine Lizzy,' I said, burning with shame for using the nickname Stamp had given her.

'No, just said hullo. She was with somebody,' he said, as though it did not matter. But it was my first bit of emotional meat this morning, and I was determined to make it matter, and to get the pain back inside where it belonged.

'Who was she with?'

'*I* don't know, I don't ask people for their autographs. What's up, are you jealous, eh? Eh?' He pronounced the word 'jealous' as though it were something he had dug up out of the garden, still hot and writhing.

The door-bell tinkled again. 'Shop,' called Arthur softly, getting up. A small woman, all the best clothes she had collected together on her body, peered round the door. 'Is this where you come to arrange for t' funerals?'

Arthur walked respectfully over to the counter.

'Ah've been in t' wrong shop. Ah thought it were next door.' She leaned heavily on the counter, her arms folded against it, and began to spell out her name.

I got up, stiffly, feeling the calendars under my pullover, and the waft of cold air when I separated them from my shirt. 'Off to the bog,' I muttered to Stamp and went downstairs among the cardboard boxes of shrouds and coffin handles. I pottered aimlessly among the wreath-cards and the bales of satin lining, looking for something worth having, and then went into the lavatory.

The lavatory at Shadrack and Duxbury's had a little shaving mirror on the door, where Shadrack could inspect his boils. More as a matter of routine than anything else, I put my tongue out and looked at it. There were some lumps at the back of my throat that I had never noticed before. Putting the subject of Liz on one side, I began putting my tongue between my fingers, seeing if the lumps got worse further down and wondering if this were the beginning of gingivitis which Stamp, with some justice, had suffered the year before. The sharp pain in my chest I located as the edge of the calendars shoving against my ribs. I checked the bolt on the door again, and took the calendars out from under my pullover. They were dog-eared now, with well-established creases across the envelopes. The top one was addressed to an old mother superior at the nunnery down by the canal. I took out the calendar and folded the envelope in four, a surprising bulkiness. I rammed the envelope into my side pocket, where the passion pills were, and held the calendar in my hands, the other three firmly gripped under my arm.

There was a brown-printed page for each month. The months tore off, and at the bottom of each month was a quotation. I knew some of them by heart. *'The only riches you will take to heaven are those you give away'* – January. *'Think all you speak, but speak not all you think'* – February. *'It takes sixty muscles to frown, but only thirteen to smile. Why waste energy?'* – April. I tore the leaves off one by one and dropped them into the lavatory. When I had reached October, *'It is a gude heart that says nae ill, but a better heart that thinks none,'* I decided that that was enough for the time being and pulled the length of rough string that served for a chain. As the screwed-up pieces of paper swam around in the water I tried hurriedly to count them, January to October inclusive, ten pages, in case I had dropped one on the floor for Shadrack to find and investigate. The water resumed its own level. To my horror, about half a dozen calendar leaves, soggy and still swimming, remained. I began gnawing at my lower lip and checking the signs of panic, heart, sweaty palms, tingling ankles, like a mechanic servicing a car. I flushed the lavatory again but there was only a heavy zinking noise and a trickle of water as the ball-cock protested. I perched myself on the side of the scrubbed seat and waited, staring at the mother superior's calendar. '*Those who bring sunshine to the lives of others cannot keep it from themselves'* – November.

I could hear Councillor Duxbury clumping about upstairs, aimlessly opening drawers and counting his money. Without much effort, I drifted into Ambrosia, where the Grand Yeomanry were still limping past the war memorial, their left arms raised in salute. *'It is often wondered how the left-hand salute, peculiar to Ambrosia, originated. Accounts differ but the most widely-accepted explanation is that of the seven men who survived the Battle of Wakefield. All, by an amazing coincidence, had lost their right arms. It was necessary for them to salute their President ——* '

The stairs creaked and there were footsteps on the stone floor outside. Somebody rattled the loose knob of the lavatory door. I waited for them to go away, but I could hear the heavy breathing. I began to start up a tuneless whistling so that they would know the booth was engaged, and to back-track through my recent thoughts to check that I had not been talking to myself. The door-rattling continued.

'Someone in here,' I called.

I heard the voice of Stamp: 'What you doing, man, writing your will out?'

It was the kind of remark Gran would shout up the stairs at home. 'Naff off,' I shouted, as I would dearly have loved to shout at Gran in the same situation. Stamp began pawing at the door. If there had been a keyhole he would have been peeping through it by now.

'No writing mucky words on the walls!' he called. I did not reply. The last few words were breathless and accompanied by a scraping noise on the floor, and it was obvious that he was jumping up and down, trying to peer over the top of the door. 'Naff off, Stamp, for Christ Sake!' I called. I stood up. The soggy little balls of paper were still in the lavatory but I dared not pull the chain again while Stamp was still there. I picked up the other calendars from the floor where I had put them and stuck them back inside my pullover, trying not to let the stiff paper crackle. Outside, Stamp began grunting in what he imagined to be an imitation of a man in the throes of constipation.

'Bet you're reading a mucky book,' he said in a hoarse whisper through the door. I let him ramble on. 'Bet y'are, bet you're reading a mucky book. *"His hand caressed her silken knee* ——'" and, excited by his own fevered images, he began to mouth obscenities through the cracks in the deep green door.

There was another sound on the stairs, this time the furry padding of light suède shoes, and I could imagine the yellow socks and the chocolate-brown gaberdines that went with them. I heard the nasal, nosey voice of Shadrack: 'Haven't you anything to do upstairs, Stamp?' and Stamp, crashing his voice into second gear to simulate something approaching respect, saying: 'Just waiting to go into the toilet, Mr Shadrack.'

'Yes, it's thought that some of you spend too much time down here. Far too much time,' said Shadrack. He picked at words as other people picked at spots.

Shadrack was not the stock cartoon undertaker, although he would have made a good model for other stock cartoons, notably the one concerning the psychiatrist's couch. He was, for a start, only about twenty-five years old, though grown old with quick experience, like forced rhubarb. His general approach and demeanour was that of the second-hand car salesman, and he had in fact at one time been one in the south. He was in the undertaking business because his old man was in it before him and old Shadrack had been, so to speak, young Shadrack's first account. After that he rarely attended funerals and would indeed have found it difficult in view of the R.A.F. blazer and the canary-coloured pullover which, sported being the word, he sported. But he was useful to the firm in that, besides having inherited half of it, he could get round old ladies. He was a member of most churches in Stradhoughton and to my certain knowledge was a card-carrying Unitarian, a Baptist, a Methodist, and both High and Low Church.

'You'd better get up into the office,' I heard him say to Stamp. 'I've got to go out.'

Stamp shuffled off, murmuring inarticulate servilities. I called: 'Is that you, Mr Shadrack?'

He either did not hear or did not choose to hear, but started fidgeting among the coffin handles, just outside the lavatory door.

'Is that Mr Shadrack?'

'Yes, there's someone waiting to come in there,' he said testily.

'Shan't be a minute,' I called in the high monotone of a man hailing down from the attic. 'I was wondering if I could see you before you go out?'

'What?'

The voice I had chosen was beginning to sound ridiculous. 'Was wondering if I could *see* you, 'fore you go out.'

Shadrack called back: 'Yes, I've been thinking it's about time we had a little talk.' Perched in my cold cell, I wondered miserably what he meant by that and skimmed quickly through a condensed inventory of the things he might know about.

'Well I can't see you now, Fisher, I've got to arrange a funeral. You'll have to come back after lunch.'

Every Saturday afternoon, after the firm had closed for the day, Shadrack started messing about with a drawing-board he kept in his office. He was trying to design a contemporary coffin. So far he had not had the nerve to try and interest Councillor Duxbury in the project, the Councillor being an oak and brass fittings man, but he spent a lot of time drawing streamlined caskets, as he called them, on yellow scratch-pads. One thing he had succeeded in doing was fitting out the funeral fleet, including the hearse, with a radio system. When there was a funeral Shadrack would sit in his office saying 'Able-Peter, Able-Peter, over' into a microphone. So far as I could remember, nobody ever answered him, and I could not think what he would have said if they had, except: 'Divert funeral to Manston Lane Chapel, over.' He kept a copy of *The Loved One* in his desk, but only to get ideas.

I called: 'Righto, Mr Shadrack.' I did not know whether he had gone back upstairs or whether he was still prowling about outside. Not to take chances, I flushed the lavatory again. When the water had flowed away there were two little balls of paper still floating about. I took the thick, folded envelope out of my pocket and, my face disfigured by nausea, scooped the two soggy leaves of calendar out of the lavatory. I stuffed them inside the envelope and crammed it into my pocket. Then I unbolted the door. Shadrack was standing immediately behind it, and he glanced me up and down like a customs officer as I passed.

Upstairs, Arthur had his raincoat on, waiting to go out for coffee. Before I could speak, Stamp called: 'Here he is! Reading mucky books in the bog!' I reached for my own raincoat. Stamp shouted, hoarsely so that Shadrack could not hear downstairs, 'Let's have a read! What you got, *Lady Chatterley's Lover*?' He dived forward and began scragging me around the stomach. He felt the stiff calendars under my pullover and bellowed in triumph: 'He has! He has! He's got a mucky book under his jersey! *Coarrr!* Dirty old man!'

I seized his wrists and snapped: '*Take* your stinking mucky hands off my pullover, stupid-looking crow!'

'Give us your mucky book,' pleaded Stamp, wheezing in his joke-over way.

Arthur was twiddling the door-handle impatiently. 'Are you coming out for coffee?' I pulled my coat on.

'Don't be all day, you two, I want some,' said Stamp.

'Go to hell,' I said.

'Don't take any wooden bodies,' Arthur called from the door.

'Go to hell,' said Stamp.

Chapter Three

Stradhoughton was littered with objects for our derision. We would make fascist speeches from the steps of the rates office, and we had been in trouble more than once for doing our Tommy Atkins routine under the war memorial in Town Square. Sometimes we would walk down Market Street shouting 'Apples a pound pears' to confuse the costermongers with their leather jackets and their Max Miller patter.

The memorial vase to Josiah Olroyd in Shadrack's window always triggered off the trouble at t' mill routine, a kind of serial with Arthur taking the part of Olroyd and I the wayward son.

As we began to walk down St Botolph's Passage, Arthur struck up: 'Ther's allus been an Olroyd at Olroyd's mill, and ther allus will be. Now you come 'ere with your college ways and you want none of it!'

'But father! We must all live our lives according to our lights —— ' I began in the high-pitched university voice.

'Don't gi' me any o' yon fancy talk!' said Arthur, reflecting with suspicious accuracy the tone of the old man at breakfast. 'You broke your mother's heart, lad. Do you know that?'

'Father! The men! They're coming up the drive!'

We turned into Market Street swinging our arms from side to side like men on a lynching spree. Arthur held up an imaginary lantern.

'Oh, so it's thee, Ned Leather! Ye'd turn against me, would ye?'

In the university voice: 'Now, Leather, what's afoot?' – and before Arthur could seize the part for himself, I switched accents and got into the character of Ned Leather. 'Oh, so it's the young lord and master up from Oxford and Cambridge, is it? We'll see about thee in a minute impudent young pup!'

Arthur, piqued as always because I had got the Ned Leather dialogue for myself, dropped the routine. We walked in silence past the pork butchers and the dry-cleaning shops stuffed with yellow peg-board notices, and turned into Moorgate. I was in a fairly schizophrenic state of mind. I was looking into the distance to catch a glimpse of Liz in her green suède jacket, but at the same time tensing myself ready to meet Rita, who worked in the café where we had our morning break. Digging my hands into my pockets I could feel Stamp's little box of passion pills, and this reminded me of the Witch. I was thinking confusedly about all three of them when Arthur began clearing his throat to adjust his voice into ordinary speech. I had noticed before that when he had something unpalatable to say he would preface it with a bit of clowning from either the trouble at t' mill or Duxbury routines.

'My mother's been saying how nice it would be if our families could get together,' he said at length.

'God forbid,' I said.

A star feature of my No. 2 thinking was a morbid dread of Arthur's mother meeting *my* mother. I had once told Arthur's mother, in a loose moment, that I had a sister called Sheila.

'And she wants to send some old toys to the kids as well,' said Arthur.

'All contributions gratefully received,' I said, still flippant.

I wondered to myself why I had ever started it. In the odd bored moments, waiting for Arthur to tie his tie in the quiet ticking house where he lived, I had got Shiela married to a grocer's assistant in the market called Eric. Eric, prospering, now had three shops of his own, two in Leeds and one in Bradford. As conversation lagged between me and Arthur's mother, I had given Eric and Sheila two children: Norma, now aged three, and Michael, aged one and a half. Michael had unfortunately been born with a twisted foot, but medical skill on the part of one Dr Ubu, an Indian attached to Leeds University, had left him with a hardly noticeable limp. Arthur had often asked me to kill my sister off and put the kids in a home, but the long-drawn-out mourning and a Shadrack and Duxbury funeral were beyond me. I felt indignant that his mother should take so much interest in a family of what, after all, were total strangers to her.

'Anyway, don't let your mother come near *our* house,' I said. 'I've told 'em she's in hospital with a broken leg.' This was the truth, not the truth that Arthur's mother was in hospital, but the truth that I, to tide me over some awkward moment, had said she was.

'The trouble with you, cocker, is you're a pathological bloody liar,' said Arthur.

'Well, I've seen the psychiatrist and —— '

'Kindly leave the couch.'

We resumed our silence, this one more uncomfortable than the last. I saw that we had a hundred yards to go before the café, and I switched in to the No. 1 thinking for a brief morning bulletin. My No. 1 mother was on: 'Billy, is this another of your *ghastly* practical jokes?' The idea of switching in brought a radio into my mind, a little white portable singing among the rubber-plants on the low-slung shelves as I mixed the drinks before dinner. My No. 1 mother said: 'Do for God's sake turn off that bloody *box*!' but this brought me back to the Vim-scoured face of my actual mother and her letter to Housewives' Choice. Cornered between the Guilt Chest and the spectre of *Arthur's* mother it was with some relief that I saw that we were outside the glassy, glacial doors of the Kit-Kat café and its monstrous, wobbling plaster sundae.

The Kit-Kat was another example of Stradhoughton moving with the times, or rather dragging its wooden leg about five paces behind the times. The plaster sundae was all that was supposed to be left of a former tradition of throbbing urns, slophouse cooking, and the thin tide of biscuit crumbs and tomato pips that was symbolic of Stradhoughton public catering. The Kit-Kat was now a coffee bar, or thought it was. It had a cackling espresso machine, a few empty plant-pots, and about half a dozen glass plates with brown sugar stuck all over them. The stippled walls, although redecorated, remained straight milkbar: a kind of Theatre Royal backcloth showing Dick Whittington and his cat hiking it across some of the more rolling dales. Where the coffee bar element really fell down, however, was in the personality of Rita, on whom I was now training the sights of my anxiety. With her shiny white overall, her mottled blonde hair, and her thick red lips, she could have transmogrified the Great Northern Hotel itself into a steamy milkbar with one wipe of her tea-cloth.

'You know, dark satanic mills I can put up with,' I said

as we climbed on the wobbling stools. 'But when it comes to dark satanic power stations, dark satanic housing estates and dark satanic coffee bars —— '

'Put on another record, kid, we've heard that one before,' said Arthur in a surprisingly coarse voice.

The Kit-Kat was full of people of the Stamp variety, all making hideous puns and leaning heavily on the I've-stopped-smoking-I-do-it-every-day kind of conversation. Rita was serving chocolate Penguins to a mob of cyclists at the other end of the bar. She waved, tinkling her fingers as though playing the piano, and I waved back.

'Watch your pockets, fellers! See if they measure you up!' This was the standard greeting from the Stamp crowd for any of us from Shadrack and Duxbury's, and the reply was: 'Drop dead.' – 'Will you bury me if I do?' – 'Free of charge, mate,' and that was the end of the responses.

'No, look, seriously though, you haven't said our old woman's broken her leg, have you?' said Arthur.

'Course I have.'

'She'll go bloody bald, man! What if I'd called at your house and your old woman had asked after her?'

'You would have risen to the occasion,' I said mock-heroically.

'The liefulness is terrific,' said Arthur, entering reluctantly into the mood of banter.

I toyed with the Perspex-covered menu, advertising onion soup that did not exist. 'Think Stamp really *did* see Liz this morning?' I said.

'*I* don't bloody know, man,' Arthur said, adding irrelevantly: 'I've lost track of your sex life.'

'No, I was just wondering,' I said.

Arthur nodded furtively up the bar towards Rita, who was still engaged in primitive verbal by-play with the cyclists. 'Listen,' he whispered hoarsely. 'Which one of 'em are you supposed to be engaged to – her or the Witch?'

'That's an academic question.'

'Well you can't be engaged to them both at once, for Christ sake,' said Arthur.

I turned a wryly-haunted face to him. 'How much have you got *says* I can't?'

'Jesus wept!' said Arthur.

The position with Rita was that I had had my eye on her

ever since she moved into the Kit-Kat from a transport cafe in the Huddersfield Road, her natural habitat. A life of mechanical badinage with lorry drivers had left her somewhat low on the conversational level, but she was a good, or at least a stolid, listener. The previous night, in an eloquent mood, I had proposed marriage and Rita, probably thinking it bad manners to refuse, had accepted. The only complicated thing was that I was already engaged to the Witch, so that Rita's status was roughly that of first reserve in the matrimonial team.

'Well which one of them's got the naffing *engagement* ring?' whispered Arthur.

I said: 'Well, the Witch had it, only I've got it back. I'm supposed to be getting it adjusted at the jeweller's.' The Witch's engagement ring in its little blue box, I now remembered, was among the items of loot in my jacket pockets. I wondered in a fleeting panic what they would make of it all if I was knocked down by a bus and my possessions were sent home to Hillcrest.

'Who's next on the list – Woodbine Lizzie?' said Arthur.

'No,' I said. 'We can accept no further engagements.'

'Write that down,' said Arthur.

At the other end of the counter, Rita's conversation with the cyclists ended abruptly as one of them stumbled over the tight boundaries of propriety. She pitched her mill-tinged, masculine voice at its most raucous to call back 'Gerron home, yer mother wants yer boots for loaftins!' as she turned away and sauntered down the bar, running the gauntlet of standard raillery as she came to greet us. There was no doubt at all that the Stamp crowd had something to whistle about. Rita was a natural for every beauty contest where personality was not a factor. She had already been Miss Stradhoughton, and she had been voted The Girl We Would Most Like To Crash The Sound Barrier With by some American airmen.

Arthur slumped himself ape-fashion across the bar. 'Gimme two cawfees, ham on rye, slice blueberry pie,' he drawled, a snatch from the two Yanks in a drugstore routine which we were still perfecting.

'Oo, look what's crawled out of the cheese,' said Rita. 'Marlon Brando.'

'If I fire this rod it'll be curtains for you, sister,' said Arthur out of the side of his mouth.

'Yer, cos it's a curtain rod. Tell us summat we don't know.'

'Well come on, love, pour us a coffee,' I said, speaking for the first time.

'Gerroff yer knees,' said Rita without rancour, strolling over to the espresso machine. So far there had been no sign from anybody, her, me, or anybody else, that we were engaged to be married.

Someone out of the Stamp crowd, preparing to leave, called out: 'Coming to the Odeon tonight, Rita, back row, eh?' Without turning round she called back: 'They wun't let you in, it's an "A" picture.'

Everybody I knew spoke in clichés, but Rita spoke as though she got her words out of a slot machine, whole sentences ready-packed in a disposable tinfoil wrapper. There was little meaning left in anything she actually said; her few rough phrases had been so worn through constant use that she now relied not on words but on the voice itself, and the modulation of the animal sounds it produced, to express the few thick slabs of meaning of which she was capable. In moments of tenderness a certain gruffness, like Woodbine smoke, would curl into her throat, but she had long ago forgotten, and probably never knew, the vocabulary of human kindness.

She slopped the coffee in front of us, Joe's Café style, and rested her elbows on the counter, her bosom – itself a cliché, like a plaster relief given away by the women's magazines – protruding over the bar. She now thought it necessary to make some delicate reference to the fact that we had had a momentous time of it the night before.

'What time did you get in last night?' she said.

''Bout one o-clock,' I said. 'Our old man went crackers this morning. Should've heard him.'

'Me man did as well. I've got to stop in on Monday. Why, did you miss your bus or summat?'

'Yer – 'ad to walk,' I said, falling chameleon-like into her own tongue.

'Why didn't you take a taxi, old man, old man?' said Arthur in his Western Brothers voice.

'Oo, hark at Lord Muck,' said Rita. 'You should have gone to Town Square, got an all-night bus.'

This was the sequence and rhythm of daylight love-play

as she knew it, a kind of oral footy-footy that was the nearest she could get to intimate conversation.

'No, I like walking,' I said.

Rita said, 'Tramp, tramp, tramp, the boys are marching,' in the derisory tone she used to apologise for putting her tongue to a quotation. 'Anyway, you're lucky, you can always get your shoes mended free.'

I was puzzled by the remark until I remembered, dredging among the fallen platitudes of the night before, an invitation I had made to Rita to come to Sunday tea. The invitation had been make-weight, a kind of free coupon along with the proposal, but in the course of it I had told her that the old man was a cobbler with a shop down Clogiron Lane.

'Oh, yer,' I said. 'Are you still going to the Roxy tonight?'

'Yer.'

'Have I to see you inside, or outside?'

'Are you kidding?'

'Just thought I'd get away without paying,' I said. It was standard, ready-to-use repartee, expected and indeed sought after. 'See you outside, then 'bout nine o'clock. Are you still coming for your tea tomorrow?'

'Yer, if you like. Anyway, we'll fix that up tonight,' she said.

Rita did not know it, but the matter was already fixed. The old man would be called away to inspect a load of Government surplus rubber heels in Harrogate, my mother would take the opportunity of a lift to visit my Auntie Polly in Otley or somewhere, and the tea would be postponed. I had not yet tackled the problem of the Roxy, to which I was also supposed to be going with the Witch. Arthur, by my side, was covering his face with his hands and making quiet cawing noises in a pantomime of amazement. I gave him a quick kick on the foot and felt in my pocket for the little blue box with the Witch's engagement ring in it.

'Try this on for size,' I said, sliding it casually across the counter.

'What, is it for me?' said Rita in her gormless way.

'Who do you think it's for, your mother?'

She opened the box and put the cheap, shiny engagement ring on her finger, as though expecting a practical joke. 'Just fits,' she said grudgingly. 'Why, you haven't *bought* it, have yer?'

'No, he knocked it off out of Woolworth's window,' said Arthur, who had started whistling tunelessly and looking up at the ceiling.

'Oo, it can speak!' jeered Rita. She changed her voice to find the unfamiliar tone of gratitude. 'Anyway, ta. I *won't* wear it now, cos you know what they're like in here.' I could see the picture of marriage forming in her mind, the white wedding, the drawers crammed full of blankets, the terrace house with the linoleum squares, the seagrass stools and the novel horseshoe companion-set in satin-brass. I felt pleased to have brought her this temporary pleasure, but there was no time to lose, and already I was racing ahead with the No. 1 thinking, breaking the engagement with the big speech about incompatability.

The glass doors of the Kit-Kat rocked open, and one of the burly lorry drivers with whom Rita had had barren and wintry affairs in the past shambled in. 'Look what the cat's brought in,' said Rita loudly. She slipped the engagement ring into her overall pocket and re-set her face into gum-chewing nonchalance.

I was smiling as we walked back to the office. 'What have *you* got to grin about?' said Arthur.

'Those who bring sunshine into the lives of others cannot keep it for themselves,' I said.

'You what?'

'A quotation from Messieurs Shadrack and Duxbury's calendars,' I said. The calendars were still warm and sharp under my pullover, but they had become a part of my clothing, like an armoured vest.

'You're going to be up for bloody bigamy, mate, that's what you're going to be up for,' said Arthur.

I tried to look as though I knew more than he did about my affairs, and we walked on along Moorgate.

'Have I told you I'm leaving?' I said, putting it as casually as I could.

'Yes, we've heard that one before as well,' said Arthur.

I wondered whether to tell him at all, or whether just to vanish, turning up self-consciously in a camel-hair coat years later like somebody coming home in uniform.

'I'm going to London,' I said.

'What as – road-sweeper?'

'Ay road sweepah on the road – to fame!' I cried in the

grandiloquent voice. When it came to the point, I was embarrassed about telling him. I added, in a shuffling kind of way: 'I've got that job with Danny Boon.'

'You haven't!'

'Yup. Scriptwriter, start next week.'

'Jammy bastard! Have you though, honest?'

'Course I have. Don't tell anybody, though, will you?'

'Course I won't. When did you fix *that* up, then?' Arthur was finding it hard to keep the traces of envy out of his voice.

'He sent me a letter.'

Arthur stopped abruptly in the middle of the street and gave me what my mother would have described as an old-fashioned look.

'*Let's* see it,' he said, holding his hand out resignedly.

'What?' I remembered where I had left the letter, in the pocket of the raincoat I used for a dressing-gown, and I wondered if my mother was snooping round reading it.

'Come on – letter,' said Arthur, clicking his fingers.

'I haven't got it with me.'

'No, thought not. I'll believe it when I see it.'

'All right, you wait till next week,' I said, trying hard to get into the spirit of jocular injured innocence, but succeeding only in the injured innocence.

'What's he paying you, then?' He was as bad as my mother.

'Wait till next week.'

'No, what's he paying you?'

'Wait till next week. You don't believe me, so wait till next *week*.'

We were back in St Botolph's Passage. I started on an indignant sliver of No. 1 thinking. 'The Danny Boon Show! Script by Billy Fisher, produced by —— ' Before I could get any further with this, I detected the pale shape of Stamp, hopping about in Shadrack's doorway, making an elaborate show of tutting and looking at his watch.

'Where've you been for your coffee – Bradford?'

'No, Wakefield,' I said, bad-tempered. Stamp buttoned his splitting leather gloves.

'The Witch has been ringing up for you,' he said. 'She rang up twice. I'm off to tell Rita you're two-timing her.'

'Go to hell,' I said.

Anyway, she said if she doesn't ring back, she wants to meet you at one o'clock, usual place.'

'She'll be lucky.'

'Is she willing?' said Stamp, speaking the phrase as though it were a headline. I snarled at him, half-raising my elbow, and went into the office.

Chapter Four

At the far end of St Botolph's Passage, past the green wrought-iron urinal, was a broken-down old lychgate leading into the churchyard. St Botolph's, a dark, dank slum of a church, was the home of a Ladies' Guild, a choir, some mob called the Shining Hour and about half a dozen other organisations, but so far as I knew it had no actual congregation except Shadrack, who went there sometimes looking for trade. The churchyard itself had long ago closed for business and most of the people in it had been carried away by the Black Death. It had a wayside pulpit whose message this week was: 'It Is Better To Cry Over Spilt Milk Than To Try And Put It Back In The Bottle,' a saw that did not strike me for one as being particularly smart.

I reached the lych-gate at one o'clock, straight after work. The Witch was fond of the churchyard as a rendezvous. We had first met at the St Botolph's youth club and she was a great one for the sentimental associations. She was also very fond of the statues of little angels around the graves, which she thought beautiful. She shared with Shadrack a liking for the sloppy bits of verse over the more modern headstones. I would have liked to have seen her as Stradhoughton's first woman undertaker.

I sat down on the cracked stone bench inside the porch and collected at least some of my thoughts together. The first thing was to get the stack of creased calendars out from under my pullover. My stomach felt cramped and cold where they had been. I pulled the envelope of soggy paper gingerly out of my jacket pocket. Then I bundled the whole lot together and shoved it under the porch seat, where no one would ever look. That seemed to dispose of the calendars. I took out of my pocket the folded carbon copy of a letter I had written to Shadrack on the firm's notepaper when I got back from the Kit-Kat.

Dear Mr Shadrack,

With regret I must ask you to accept my resignation from Shadrack and Duxbury's. You probably know that while enjoying my work with the Firm exceedingly, I have always regarded it as a temporary career. I have now succeeded in obtaining a post with Mr Danny Boon, the London comedian, and I do feel that this is more in line with my future ambitions.

I realise that you are entitled to one week's notice, but under the circumstances I wonder if it would be possible to waive this formality. May I say how grateful I am for all the help you have given me during my stay with the Firm.

My best personal regards to yourself and Councillor Duxbury.

I was rather pleased with the letter, especially the bit about being grateful for Shadrack's help, but still apprehensive about the interview it would be necessary to have with him when I had finished with the Witch. I speculated idly on what he was getting at by saying it was about time we had a little talk. I looked out at the church clock and thought: never mind, in one hour it will all be over. I put the letter away again and began thinking about the Witch, the slow and impotent anger brewing up as it always did whenever I dwelt on her for any length of time.

The point about the Witch was that she was completely sexless. She was large, clean, and as I knew to my cost, wholesome. I had learned to dislike everything about her. I did not care, to begin with, for her face: the scrubbed, honest look, as healthy as porridge. I disliked her for her impeccable shorthand, her senseless, sensible shoes and her handbag crammed with oranges. The Witch did nothing else but eat oranges. She had in fact been peeling a tangerine when I proposed to her during a youth club hike to Ilkley Moor, and her way of consummating the idea had been to pop a tangerine quarter in my mouth. She had not been very much amused when I said: 'With this orange I thee wed.'

What I most disliked her for were the sugar-mouse kisses and the wrinkling-nose endearments which she seemed to think symbolised some kind of grand passion. I had already cured her of calling me 'pet lamb' by going 'Jesus H. Christ!' explosively when she said it. The Witch had said sententiously: 'Thou shalt not take the name of the Lord thy God in vain.' I disliked her for her sententiousness, too.

Part of the booty in my raincoat pockets was a dirty, crumpled bag of chocolates that had been there for months. I had bought them when Stamp handed over his white box of passion pills. 'You'll need necking fodder to go with them,' he had explained. I took the chocolates out and inspected them. There had originally been a quarter of a pound, but as one opportunity after another slipped by, I had started to eat the odd chocolate and now there were only three left at the bottom of the bag, squashed and pale milky brown where they had melted and re-set.

I put the paper bag on my knee. Fumbling about in my side pocket I found Stamp's little box. That too was squashed almost flat by now, and most of the pills had rolled out into my pocket. I took one out, a little black bead that looked inedible. I wondered again where Stamp had got them and why he had given them to me, and also whether I could be prosecuted for what I was doing. 'Fisher, pay attention to me.' I fished around for the most presentable chocolate I could find, and tried to break it in half. It would not break properly. The chocolate covering splintered like an eggshell. It was an orange cream. I stuffed the round little black bead into it and tried to press the chocolate whole again. The result was a filthy, squalid mess. I ate one of the remaining chocolates, and then the second, leaving only the doctored orange cream in its grimy paper bag.

I lit a cigarette and stood up, and stretched. Looking down St Botolph's Passage, I saw the Witch picking her way disdainfully through the swaying little groups of betting men who were beginning to congregate.

I felt the usual claustrophobia coming on as she marched up to the lych-gate, swinging her flared skirt like a Scot swings his kilt; an arrogant and not a sexy swing. I disliked the way she walked.

'Hullo,' the Witch said, coldly. She was always cold whenever we were anywhere that resembled a public place. Later on she would start the ear-nibbling, the nose-rubbing and the baby talk. I said: 'Hullo, dalling.' I could not say darling. I was always trying, but it always came out as dalling.

We sat down together on the hard stone bench, under the spiders' webs. She eyed my Player's Weight viciously.

'How many cigarettes today?'

'Two,' I said.

'That's a good boy,' the Witch said, not quite half jokingly. She had got hold of some idea that I was smoking only five a day.

'Did you have a busy morning, dalling?' I said, giving her the soulful look. The Witch raised her eyeballs and blew upwards into her nostrils, a habit for which I was fast getting ready to clout her.

'Only about thirty letters from Mr *Turn*bull. Then he wanted me to type out an ag*ree*ment . . .' She rattled on in this vein for a few minutes.

'Did you talk to any *men* today?' I asked her. This was another idea she had. I was supposed to be jealous if she spoke to anybody else but me.

'Only Mr Turnbull, and Stamp when I rang up. Did you talk to any *gurls*?'

'Only the waitress when we went out for coffee.'

The Witch put on a mean expression. 'Couldn't your friend have spoken to her?' she pouted. She wouldn't speak Arthur's name, because even *that* was supposed to make me jealous.

'Dalling!' I said. 'Have you missed me?'

'Of course. Have you missed *me*?'

'Of course.'

That seemed to be the end of the inquisition. I grubbed around in my pocket and produced what was left of the chocolates. 'I saved this for you,' I said.

The Witch peered doubtfully into the sticky, brown-stained depths of the paper bag.

'It looks a bit *squashed*,' she said.

I took the chocolate between my fingers. 'Open wide.' She opened her mouth, probably to protest, and I rammed the chocolate in.

'Nasty!' said the Witch, gulping. I craned my neck, pretending to scratch my ear, and glanced out of the porch at the church clock. Stamp's passion pills were supposed to take effect after a quarter of an hour at most. He had once given me a description of a straight-laced, straight-faced Baloo who ran a Wolf Cub pack over in Leeds, and she had started pawing his jacket and whimpering only five minutes after he had slipped her a passion pill in the guise of an energy tablet.

'What were you ringing up about this morning? Anything?'

'Just wanted to talk to you, pet,' said the Witch, wriggling herself into a position of squeamish luxury. 'I've seen the most marvellous material to make curtains for our cottage. Honestly, you'll love it.'

Eating oranges in St Botolph's churchyard on the long crisp nights, or sometimes in the public shelter at the Corporation cemetery, another favourite spot, we had discussed at length the prospect of living in a thatched cottage in the middle of some unspecified field in Devon. At times, in the right mood, I could get quite enthusiastic over this rural image, and it had even figured in my No. 1 thinking before now. We had invented two children, little Barbara and little Billy – the prototypes, actually, of the imaginary family I had told Arthur's mother about – and we would discuss their future, and the village activities and the pokerwork mottoes and all the rest of it.

'It's a sort of turquoise, with lovely little squiggles, like wine-glasses —— '

'Will it go with the yellow carpet?'

'No, but it'll go with the grey rugs in the kiddies' room.'

'Dalling!'

The yellow carpet and the grey rugs we had seen in a furniture shop window on one of the interminable expeditions round Stradhoughton that the Witch sometimes dragged me on. They had all long ago been sold, but they had become part of the picture of the cottage, along with the Windsor chairs, the kettle singing on the hob, the bloody cat and also the crinoline ladies from my bedroom wall at home.

We continued on these lines for a few minutes, until, at a reference to the wedding ceremony in some village church that would precede it all, the Witch stiffened.

'Have you got my engagement ring back yet?'

'Not yet, crikey! I only took it in this morning!' The Witch had parted with it suspiciously and reluctantly, not really convinced that it needed making smaller.

'I feel unclothed without it,' she said. She could not bring herself to say 'naked,' yet from her, 'unclothed' sounded even more obscene than she imagined nakedness to be. The reference reminded me that her time was nearly up.

'Let's go in the churchyard, away from all the people,' I said, standing up and taking her cold, chapped hands.

She looked, doubtful again, into the dead-looking graveyard. 'It's a bit *damp*, isn't it?'

'We'll sit on my raincoat. Come on, dalling.' I was almost dragging her to her feet. She got up half-heartedly. I put my arm around her awkwardly, and we walked up the broken tarmacadam path that was split down the middle like the crust on a cottage loaf, round to the back of the old church. Behind some ancient family vault was a black tree and a clump of burnt-looked, dirty old grass. Sometimes I could persuade the Witch to sit down there, when she was not inspecting the vault and reading out aloud: 'Samuel Vaughan of this town, 1784; alfo his wife Emma, alfo his fon Saml, 1803.' I threw my raincoat on the shoddy grass and sat down. The Witch remained standing and I pulled her impatiently, almost forcibly, to her knees. By now, even allowing extra time for a difficult case, Stamp's pill should be working.

I stared at her gravely. 'I love you, dalling,' I said in the stilted way that I couldn't help.

'Love *you*,' said the Witch, the stock response which she imagined the statement needed.

'Do you? Really and truly?'

'Of course I do.'

'Are you looking forward to getting married?'

'I think about it every minute of the day,' she said. I disliked the way she talked, tempering her flat northern voice with the mean, rounded vowels she had picked up at the Stradhoughton College of Commerce.

'Dalling,' I said. I began stroking her hair, moving as quickly as possible down the side of her face and on to her shoulder. She started the nose-rubbing act, and I seized her roughly and began kissing her. My lips on hers, I decided that I might as well try to get my tongue into her mouth but she kept her lips hard and closed. She pulled her face away suddenly so that my tongue slithered across her cheek and I was licking her, like a dog. It was not a very promising start.

'Don't ever fall in love with anybody else,' I said in the grave, sad voice. 'Love you pet,' she said, leaning forward and nibbling my ear. I caught hold of her again and started fumbling, as idly as I could manage it, at the square buttons on her neat blue suit. The Witch struggled free again.

'Let's talk about our cottage, pet,' she said.

I counted seven to myself, seeing the red rash in front of my eyes. Obviously the pill was not working yet, or perhaps in the Witch's case I should have given her three of four.

'What about our cottage?' I said in the dreamy voice, containing myself.

'About the garden. Tell me about the garden.'

'We'll have a lovely garden,' I said, conjuring up a garden without much trouble. 'We'll have rose trees and daffodils and a lovely lawn with a swing for little Billy and little Barbara to play on, and we'll have our meals down by the lily pond in summer.'

'Do you think a lily pond is *safe*?' the Witch said anxiously. 'What if the kiddies wandered too near and fell in?'

'We'll build a wall round it. No we won't, we won't have a pond at all. We'll have an old well. An old brick well where we draw the water. We'll make it our wishing well. Do you know what I'll wish?'

The Witch shook her head. She was sitting with her hands folded round her ankles like a child being told a bedtime story.

'Tell me what you'll wish, first,' I said.

'Oh – I'll wish that we'll always be happy and always love each other. What will *you* wish?' the Witch said.

'Better not tell you,' I said.

'Why not, pet?'

'You might be cross.'

'Why would I be cross?'

'Oh, I don't know. You might think me too, well, forward.' I glanced at her face for reaction. There was no reaction, and in fact when I looked at her again she seemed to have lost interest in the wishing well. I tried the lip-biting trick, combined with the heavy breathing.

'Barbara —— ' I began, making a couple of well-feigned false starts. 'Do you think it's wrong for people to have, you know, feelings?'

The Witch looked at me, too directly for my liking. 'Not if they're genuinely in love with each other,' she said.

'Like we are?'

'Yes,' she said, with less certainty.

'Would you think it wrong of me to have – feelings?'

The Witch, speaking briskly and firmly as though she had been waiting for this one and knew what to do about it, said: 'I think we ought to be married first.'

I looked at her sorrowfully. 'Dalling.' I got hold of the back of her neck and kissed her again. This time, making a bold decision, I put my hand on the thick, salmon-coloured stocking, just about at the shin. She stiffened, but did not do anything about it. I moved the hand up, the voice of Stamp floating into my mind. *'His hand caressed her silken knee.'* As soon as I reached her knee the Witch tore herself free.

'Are you feeling all right?' she said abruptly.

'Of course, dalling. Why?' I said, not moving my hand.

She looked pointedly down at her knee. 'Look where your hand is.'

I moved it away, sighing audibly.

'Dalling, don't you *want* me to touch you?'

The Witch shrugged.

'It seems – indecent, somehow.' I leaned forward to kiss her again, but she side-stepped abruptly, reaching for the leather shoulder-bag that she always carried with her.

'Would you like an energy tablet?' I said.

'No, thank you. I'm going to have an orange.'

I saw the red rash again and felt the old, impotent rage. I jumped to my feet. '*Ai'm* going to have an *or-r*ainge!' I mimicked in a falsetto voice. '*Ai'm* going to have an *or*-ainge!' On a sudden urge I booted the leather handbag out of her hand and across the grass. It came to rest by an old gravestone, spilling out oranges and shorthand dictionaires.

'Billy!' said the Witch sharply.

'You and your bloody oranges,' I said.

She sat there looking straight in front of her, obviously wondering whether it was going to be worth her while to start crying. I bent down and touched her hair.

'Sorry, dalling,' I said. I put on a shamefaced look and slunk off after her handbag. I started collecting her oranges and things together, looking closely into her open handbag to see if there were any letters from men I might be able to use. There was nothing but her lipstick and a few coins, but on the grass close by I saw something small and gleaming. I recognised it as a miniature silver cross that the Witch used to wear around her neck. Until a few months ago she had never been without it, then she had revealed that it was a present from some cousin called Alec who lived in Wakefield. Under the jealousy pact between us I had made her promise to give it back to him, and according to her story she had done so.

I looked back sharply at the Witch, but she was occupied, dabbing at her eyes with her handkerchief. I slipped the little silver cross quickly into my pocket, picked up her handbag, and strolled back to where she was sitting.

'Sorry, dalling,' I said again. She reached up and squeezed my hand, sniffing deeply to prove that she had finished crying.

'Let's go,' she said.

'All right.'

We walked back along the crumbling church path, through the lych-gate and into St Botolph's Passage. I was beginning to say, 'You know, dalling, I think you have feelings too, deep down,' but the Witch had already resumed the formal attitude she assumed for public appearances. I let the matter drop.

'Are we going looking at the shops this afternoon?' she said as we paused at the corner of Market Street.

My heart sank. On Saturdays, as well as taking her to the Roxy at night, I was expected to meet her two or three times during the day – at lunch-time, during the afternoon, and possibly before I went to the pub for my club turn in the evening. She always said it made her feel wanted, although she had little idea what I wanted her for.

Today I was hoping to get out of the afternoon session.

'I'd love to, only I've got to go and see Shadrack this afternoon, and I don't know what time I'll get through.'

'Please?' She would have said 'Pretty please' if she had had the nerve.

'All right, dalling. About four o'clock. Only wait for me if I'm late.'

'All right, pet.'

Fingering her little silver cross in my raincoat pocket, I watched her down Market Street until her swinging skirt was out of sight.

Chapter Five

In the cold sun, on a Saturday afternoon, St Botolph's Passage was just about bearable. It was alive with fat men in dark suits, puffing and blowing over folded racing papers and chucking clean, empty packets of twenty down on the uneven paving stones. Men in raincoats came and went in the vicinity of the shady chemist's, and a swaying, red-faced group continued an argument outside the pub, one of them saying the same sentence over and over again like a blocked gramophone. It seemed to be the same group every Saturday, having the same argument. 'Have you ever realised,' I said to Man o' the Dales – puff, puff – 'that your blunt Yorkshire individuals are in fact interchangeable, like spare wheels on a mass-produced car?' At the end of the Passage, by Market Street, there was even a violinist with his hat on the floor, playing 'Pennies from Heaven'. Shadrack and Duxbury's was the only shop with the blinds down, but the door was open and the bell rang quietly when I went in.

The office was cold and dusty now, and looking more like a funeral parlour than usual with the roller blind filtering a green, dead light over the empty desks. I stood hesitating, gaping dozily at the washed-looking photograph of Councillor Duxbury doffing his bowler in front of a horse-driven hearse. It was very quiet. I had a quick, happy notion that they had abandoned the office for ever, or dropped dead in their own coffins or something, but then I saw the thin red glow of the convector heater shining under Shadrack's door. I went over reluctantly and knocked. He was not there. It was probable that he was out in Market Street, selling a Morris Thousand to some fruiterer or other. Shadrack had never quite abandoned his previous trade.

I sauntered over to my desk and sat down heavily, feeling happier because Shadrack was not there. It was, after all, not beyond the range of possibility that he had been run over by a bus. I lit one of my cigarettes and aimlessly opened the drawer of my desk. I stared vacantly into it for a moment, and then made a decision. My desk drawer was a sort of town branch of the Guilt Chest; there were few documents in it that did not cause even a passing spasm of anxiety. I began, briskly, to sort through them, tearing up the unposted funeral accounts first, then the obscene verses about Councillor Duxbury, and the rough notes for a long love letter I had once written to the Witch, daringly mentioning her breasts by name. There were about eight first pages of *The Two Schools at Gripminster.* I stacked them together, tore them through the middle, and dropped them in the wastepaper basket. There seemed to be whole sheafs of quarto with nothing written on them but my name in a variety of handwriting styles. I threw those away too. There was a fragment of dialogue entitled *Burglar Scene*, that I had once thought just right for Danny Boon:

BOON: If I fire this rod it'll be curtains for you.
FEED: W-why?
BOON: It's a curtain rod. Of course, I'm a very respectable man, you know, a very respectable man. My wife and I are in the iron and steel business.
FEED: . . .
BOON: She does the ironing while I do the stealing.

I put this in my pocket together with the beginnings of the letter I had tried to write to Danny Boon. At the back of the drawer there was an old, yellowing piece of foolscap on which I had tried to list all the things that were worrying me at the time. The idea was that I should tick off each item as it ceased to be an anxiety, and when I had finished there would be nothing left to worry me any more.

I looked at the list again, apprehensively. 'Cal. Witch (Capt). Ldn. Hswvs Choice. Namepl. A's ma (sister).' There was nothing on the long list that I could honestly cross off and forget about. I made a decision, and ripped the piece of paper into four, dropping the pieces in the wastepaper basket. There was nothing left in the desk except the long ink stain, the stubs of pencil, and the word 'LIZ' which I had blocked in in careful crayon. I got up and tried to open Stamp's desk, but it was locked. I paced round the office, whistling through my teeth.

One of the habits I was going to get out of was a sort of

vocal equivalent of the nervous grimace, an ever-expanding repertoire of odd noises and sound effects that I would run through in time of tension. Alone in my bedroom, seeking refuge in a telephone box, or walking purposefully, purposelessly home along Clogiron Lane late at night, I would begin to talk to myself, the words degenerating first into senseless, ape-like sounds and then into barnyard imitations, increasing in absurdity until I was completely incoherent, thereupon I would switch back into human speech with a kind of thought-stream monologue on whatever problem was uppermost in my mind at the time.

I did this now, dropping my cigarette end into Stamp's inkwell.

'London is a big place, Mr Shadrack,' I began, mumbling to myself. 'A man can lose himself in London. You know that? Lose himself. Loo-hoo-hoose himself. Loooooooose himself. Himself. Him, himmmmnnn, himnnn, himself. Ah-him-ah-self! Wandering about the office, I started on the odd sounds and the imitations of animals. 'Hyi! Hyi! Yi-yi-yi-yi-yi. Grrruff! Grrruff! Maaa-aaa Maa-aaa! *Maaaaa!* And now —— ' – taking in a fragment of one of the routines I went through with Arthur from time to time – 'and now as Sir Winston *Chur*chill might have said it. Nevah! In the field! Of human conflict! And this is the voiceofemall, Wee Willy Fisher, saying maa-aaa! Maaaa! Maaaaa! Grmp. Grmp. What a beautiful little pig. Hay say, whhat ay *beau*tiful little pig.' I began to repeat this sentence in a variety of tones, stresses and dialects, ranging from a rapid Mickey Mouse squeak to a bass drawl, and going through all the Joycean variations. 'What a batiful lattle pahg. Ah, whet eh behtefell lettle peg.'

I was standing at the open door of Shadrack's office. The room was beginning to echo with my voice. I stopped for a moment and toyed with the idea of going in and having a quick run through Shadrack's desk, but my ankles tingled at the thought. I had a short flash of No. 2 thinking, trapped in Shadrack's swivel chair with the drawer of his desk jammed open. For relief, I turned back to my verbal doodling and began to call his name.

'Mr Shadrack? Mr Shadrack? Ha-*mees*ter Shadrack! Meehee-heester Shadrack! Shadrack! Shadrack!' Each time I called, the 'rack' sound bounced back off his streamlined convector stove. '*Shad*rack! Shar-har-har-har-*had*rack! Shaddy-shaddy-shaddy-shaddy-*shad*rack! Hoy! Shadders!'

I was just drawing breath for the second run when Shadrack, who had undoubtedly been listening for the past ten minutes, came into the office through the door that led down to the lavatory. I stuck a finger in my throat and began going 'Ar! Ar! Arrrgh! Sharrgh!' trying to falsify his memory of what he had heard. My first real thought was one of relief that I had not been going through his desk; my second was to turn on him the Ambrosian repeater gun, rather like a machine-gun, which I kept permanently manned for such occasions as this.

'Oh, it's you, is it?' said Shadrack, but without any indication that these words explained, or excused, the din I had been making. Had he heard everything, or had he just come up from downstairs? Even downstairs he could not have failed to hear. Four moves flashed through my mind like a drowning man's life story. One, pretend was singing. Two, pretend not seen him and continue, making it sound like singing. Three, pretend rehearsing play. 'And yet, Lady Alice, even pigs have feelings.' Four, on the No. 1 level, 'I'm glad you heard that, Shadrack. I've been wanting you to hear my views for a long time.'

'Hope my singing didn't put you off,' I said.

'Curious din you were making,' said Shadrack. 'You'd better come into the office.

I followed him into his private sanctum, humming in an embarrassed way.

Shadrack's office was furnished in what he imagined to be American executive style, in so far as he could afford it. He had a metal desk completely free of everything except a black ebony ruler, an unacceptable object to me ever since he had discovered me, or I think discovered me, conducting with it from a record of 'Abide With Me' which he kept on the record-player, another item of luxury. I turned the Ambrosian repeater gun on him again for good measure. On a low, coffee-bar sort of table there were the plans and drawings of the glass-fibre coffin he was working on, and a yellow pad on which he was doodling his ideas for a streamlined hearse. Beyond this, a couple of grey contemporary chairs, the first ever seen in Stradhoughton, and on the wall a boxed print of one of those Chinese horses.

'Come in, siddown, make 'self at home,' said Shadrack. He smiled with his bad teeth, and produced from his blazer pocket a matchbox-sized model, made out of Perspex, of his wedge-shaped coffin. 'Y'know, by the time we're burying you, you'll be going off in one o' these. You know that?'

'Really?' I said, trying to sound interested. I was not fooled by his manner, the well-known friendly word, the boss relaxing on his Saturday afternoon off. I perched on one of the grey chairs and cleared my throat. 'Arrgh! Sharrgh!'

'Y'see, people don't realise. It's all clean lines nowadays. All these frills and fancies are going out. It's all old.'

'H'm,' I said.

'Same as I tell Councillor Duxbury. You've got to move with the times. It's no use living in one style and dying in another. It's an anarchism.'

'Anachronism,' I said, before I could stop myself.

'Yes, well.' Shadrack turned abruptly to the olive-green filing cabinet and took out a manilla file. He held it up and tapped it. 'Anyway, that's my worry. S'pose you want to talk to me about this letter of yours, do you?' I had an absurd feeling of importance that I should have written a letter and that he should have put it in a file. He put the file, open, on the desk, and I saw that there were several other papers underneath my letter of resignation. I fell to wondering if this was some kind of personal dossier, filled with reports from Stamp and the Witch, and secret spidery mumblings from Councillor Duxbury.

Shadrack perched on his desk, adjusting his tapered slacks and shooting his cuffs. 'So y're thinking of leaving us, hey, is that it?'

'Yes, well, I *was* thinking, now this opportunity's come up . . .' I trotted out a wretched, shambling imitation of the speech I had prepared.

Shadrack picked up my letter and examined it. I tried to see what the next paper on the file was. It was one of his yellow memo-sheets with a lot of his writing on it. He frowned over the letter as though he could not read.

'". . . now succeeded in obtaining a post with Mr Danny Boon . . ."' he quoted, and I had an idea that he was going to go through the letter, point by point, getting me to expand. 'Now that's the chap who was on telly the other night, isn't it?'

'That's right,' I said in the encouraging voice.

'Yes, vair vair clever fellow. And you say you're going to work for him?'

'Yes, well, he liked some of the material I sent him and ——'

'That's your ambition is it, script-writing?' He was the eager questioner, off-duty, Saturday afternoon.

'Oh, yes, always has been,' I said, beginning to relax and sit back in my chair. 'And of course, there's quite a lot of money in it if you go about it the right way.'

'You get paid by the joke, then, or what? Or do you get a salary coming in each week?'

'Well, it's vair difficult to say,' I said. I had noticed before that I often tended to start imitating the person I was talking to. But Shadrack had lost interest. While I was scrabbling away trying to think of something to tell him, he began murmuring. 'Ye-es, ye-es' absent-mindedly and shuffling the papers in the file. His expression changed to a business one. He got up off the desk and stood behind his chair, putting his full weight on it and swivelling it from side to side.

'Ye-es. Well this letter,' Shadrack began, and it was obvious that we were getting down to the serious business. I looked up intelligently.

'Now you don't need me to tell you that it's vair vair unsatisfactory, a letter like this. Now do you?'

I mumbled, trying to get some action into my voice: 'Oh, I'm sorry to hear that?'

'Vair unsatisfactory. Fact I'd go so far as to say it's unprofessional, Fisher. Vair vair unprofessional.'

Shadrack had a thing about the undertaking business being a profession. I cleared my throat and said: 'Well, I suppose I've got to leave some time —— '

'Yes, we realise that. We all realise that. Don't doubt it. Nobody wants to stand in your way, don't think that, and I wish you the vair vair best of luck. But it's felt that you might have gone about it in a more sa'sfactory manner.'

'Oh, in what way?' It sounded like something out of amateur dramatics, the way I said it.

'Well we were hoping, we were *hoping*, that you'd try and get one or two things cleared up before you took a step like this.'

An icy chill, a familiar enough visitor by now, seized me

somewhere under the heart. I cleared my throat again and said faintly: 'What —— ?'

'Y'see, I don't mind telling you that we're vair vair disappointed you've not been to see us *before* this. I mean before you wrote this letter. I mean don't think I want to make things *awk*ward for you, far from it, but it has been felt you owe us one or two little explanations.'

I was difficult not to look as though I understood what he was talking about. I said, trying to keep up the equal partners voice of a few moments before, 'Well, I know my work probably hasn't been as good as it might have been. I mean, that's one of the reasons why I think I ought to leave.'

'It's not a question of work,' said Shadrack. 'It's not a question of work at all. It's just a question of what you pr'pose to do about one or two things.'

He looked at me levelly, trying to gauge how much of the message was coming across. Then he said, almost gently: 'Y'see, there's those calendars to be explained, for one thing. I mean, we've never had any sa'sfactory explanation about *that*, now have we?'

I stared back at him, licking my lips. It was no surprise to me that Shadrack actually knew about the calendars. He was bound to suspect, if not to know. I had just been hoping that natural delicacy or some kind of feeling of hopelessness would have prevented him from bringing the subject up. There were many things, in fact, on which I leaned heavily on the reluctant, brooding tact that was Shadrack's speciality. I decided that my best policy was to say nothing, and indeed I had nothing to say.

'I mean, they cost a lot of money to produce, a *lot* of money. We can't understand what you did with them.'

I felt bound to make some sort of effort. 'Well, there was a bit of a misunderstanding —— ' I began, a story about a fire at the post office beginning to cobble itself together in my mind.

'It wasn't a misunderstanding, it's just that two or three hundred calendars didn't get posted. To *my* knowledge. I mean, I know you want to leave, I think it's the best thing you could do. I think you're taking a very wise step. We all realise that. But y'see, we've got to get this cleared up and implemented.'

I didn't know, and neither did he, what he meant by

'implemented'. Shadrack had a habit of hoarding words and dropping them into a sentence when they got too heavy for him. It was obvious now that he was going to go on and on about the calendars, probably for half the afternoon, simply because he had never studied the art of hanging the subject. I decided that I was supposed to make some constructive suggestion.

'Well, of course, if it's a question of paying for them ——'

'Ah. Aha! Wait a minute. Wait just one little minute. It's not as easy as that. It's not – as easy as that. Y'see, there's the goodwill to consider. What about the goodwill? Those calendars were for goodwill, we can't understand why you didn't send them out. I mean that's what they're there for. I mean, we don't buy calendars so that you can just go out and chuck them on the fire, y'know. That's not what we're in business for.'

He was getting warmed up now. He had stopped fiddling about with his chair and was sitting down, leaning forward over the desk, messing about with the ebony ruler. His eyes glistened.

'No, that won't do at all. I'm afraid you don't seem to apprec'ate it's a vair vair serious business. And then of course there's the other matter.'

'What other matter?' I said dully.

'I think you know vair well what matter. It's no good sitting there saying what matter. There's this matter of the nameplates, isn't there?'

Here I had no advantage at all, and for the first time my mouth sagged. I had suspected, when I considered the thing seriously, that Shadrack knew about the calendars. I felt that he knew something about the irregularities in the postage book, a subject I was surprised had not been ventilated earlier in the conversation. I was fairly sure that he knew about the offensive imitations of Councillor Duxbury but was too inarticulate to mention them. But I would have sworn, willingly, that he knew nothing about the nameplates.

In a way, the nameplates were just as serious as the calendars, if not more so. There were two of them, and I had hidden them in a box of shrouds down in the stockroom. The whole thing had happened during Shadrack's holiday in the summer. I had been supposed to order a coffin nameplate for the funeral of a preacher who had dropped dead in the aisle at Bridle Street Methodist Church. By mistake, thinking about something else, I had put the letters 'R.I.P.' on the engravers' instructions, with the result that they had turned out what was in effect a Catholic nameplate for a Methodist body. I had got the thing hurriedly remade, but too late for the funeral. By a miracle neither Councillor Duxbury nor the relatives had noticed it was missing, and the Methodist minister had been buried in an unidentified coffin. There was nothing to do with the nameplates but hide them, and I had often worried about them, sometimes going into the theological aspects of the affair and wondering if I had committed anything to do with the unforgivable sin. But I would have sworn that Shadrack knew nothing about it.

'Y'see, that's another matter we've got to get cleared up. I don't see how you can leave without getting *that* cleared up.'

He did not make it evident whether or not he knew where the nameplates were. Perhaps he knew only that the body had been buried without a nameplate. I had lived in fear, for some time, of an exhumation order. I decided to sneak downstairs when he let me go and stuff the nameplates under my pullover.

'Well, I can only say I'm sorry if there's been any inconvenience,' I said.

'Incon*ve*nience? Incon*ve*nience? Ha!' He gave a short snort, and entered one of his caves of rhetoric. 'It's not a question of inconvenience, it's a question of what you pr'pose to do about it. S'posing the relatives had found out, what sort of fool d'y'think I'd have looked then? S'posing Councillor Duxbury had found out?' (I felt a slight ray of hope that he was shielding me from Councillor Duxbury.) 'Y'see, I'm vair much afraid that you've been spending too much time acting the fool. You seem to think you're on the music halls, not in a funeral furnishers.'

I was beginning to be possessed by the inward, impotent rage. What did the man want me to *do*? Atone for my sins? Work for another year as penal servitude? Pay for the calendars and the nameplates? Get the goodwill back?

Shadrack looked at the yellow paper in his file where, I was quite ready to believe, he had a list of my misdemeanours scribbled down, like a charge sheet. I expected him to tick them off and start each charge with 'That he did unlawfully . . .'

'Yes, there's been too much acting the fool in this office. We'll have to get some other system. Y'see, then there's those verses, you never wrote *those* out, now did you?'

Shadrack had once caught Arthur and me writing songs in the firm's time, and had set us to work making up little verses for the In Memoriam column of the *Echo*, a chore he handled for the bereaved on a commission basis. The nearest we had got to the job was an obscene poem about Councillor Duxbury and a couple of lines about Josiah Olroyd in the window: 'Josiah Olroyd has gone to join his Maker. Come inside and join Josiah Olroyd.' Shadrack knew about them both. I was relieved that he was getting on to the minor misdemeanours, but I knew that even those could keep him talking for hours.

'Then there's all that office paper you've been using for your bits and pieces. I mean, that costs money as well.'

'I'll pay for it.'

'It's not a question of paying for it ——' In the outer office, the telephone began to ring. Shadrack picked up his extension and found that it was not connected. It was my responsibility to see that it was, last thing on Saturday morning, and he shot me a look of exasperation as he rose to his feet.

'Anyway, under the circumstances I have to tell you, I have to tell *you*, Fisher, that under no circ'stances can we accept your resignation at the moment. Not at the moment. Not until we've got this straightened out. We may even have to take some kind of legal action, I don't know.'

He strode out of his office and went over to the switchboard. 'Shadrack and Duxbury?' I got up and stood in the doorway, running over the bit about legal action and testing it for strength.

Shadrack began talking to some mourning wife in his soupy, funeral voice. I just stood there. He put his hand over the mouthpiece and said: 'Well we'll talk about this another time.' I walked unsteadily to the outer door, twisted the door-handle for a moment, and walked out into St Botolph's Passage. For the first time since breakfast I felt my elusive yawn coming on, and I leaned against Shadrack's window, gasping and gulping. My forehead was sweating, but I was relieved that I had jumped another hurdle. I remembered that I had not gone downstairs after the nameplates, but decided that after all there was little point in it.

I lit a cigarette and started walking down towards Market Street, trying to translate the interview into No. 1 thinking. 'Now look here, Mr Shadrack, there's such a thing as slander ——'

It didn't work. I set off home. My No. 1 mother said: 'For God's sake, Billy, why don't you tell the boring little man what he can do with the job?'

Chapter Six

I reached Hillcrest at about half-past two to find lunch over and my mother in the kitchen, making notes for a scene about my not being home for meals. It was bacon and egg again, the traditional Saturday feast; the eggshells were in the sink-tidy and there was an air of replete doom about the house. Gran was mumbling to herself in the lounge. The old man was mending something in the garage, or thought he was.

'What time do you call this?' my mother asked as I opened the kitchen door. I knew my part in this little passage and replied: 'Twenty-seven minutes past two, though you may have another phrase for it,' reflecting that my answers were becoming as stereotyped as her questions. 'I've had an exciting morning,' I added, trying to get some uplift into the conversation.

My mother was not having any. 'You seem to think I've nothing else to do but cook, cook, cook,' she said, slipping with disturbing ease into a monologue so familiar to me that I could have chanted it with her, like those two men doing imitations on the radio. 'You come in when you like and expect to find a meal waiting for you, you don't seem to think I'm entitled to five minutes' peace.'

'Peace —— ' I began, not troubling to think what I was going to say; anything obscure would pass for something clever. My mother cut me short.

'I've not sat down all morning. If I'm not sick!'

From the lounge, Gran shouted: 'If that's our Billy, there's his old raincoat been in the bathroom all morning. It's about time he started hanging his things up.'

I called back: 'What if it isn't our Billy, where has his old raincoat been then?' a grammatical pleasantry whose full subtlety I did not expect to be appreciated. I anticipated, and got, no reply. The old man came into the kitchen from the garage, carrying a shelf.

'And you can start coming home on a dinner-time, instead

of gadding round town half the bloody day,' he said, without even looking at me.

'Good afternoon, father,' I said with heavy civility. I was beginning to wonder why I had come home at all.

'And stop being so bloody cheeky. I've just about had enough of it.'

'He wants to give him a good hiding, teach him some manners,' called Gran from the lounge.

I began to feel angry, like a caged animal being taunted with sticks. This feeling, a regular enough occurrence in this house, had several outlets. One course open to me was to revert to what I felt must be my former self or my real self or something, an abusive shadow of the old man. Another, less dangerous move was to introduce the mood of polished detachment.

'What are manners —— ?' I began, examining my fingernails. But I had underestimated the strength of the old man's frustration or whatever it was.

'Talk bloody sense, man!' he roared. 'By Christ, if this is what they learned him at technical school, I'm glad I'm bloody ignorant!'

'Ah, a confession!' I murmured, but without any idea that he should hear me. The old man gave me a steady, threatening look. Aloud, I said, 'I'm going upstairs.'

'And keep out of them bedrooms!' Gran called from the lounge.

The bedrooms were nothing to do with her. She was only the permanent guest. I whipped round in a sudden gust of fury.

'*Mind your own bloody* —— ' I began, then checked myself on the absolute verge of disaster, so abruptly that I physically teetered on my toes.

'You what!' The old man dropped his shelf on the floor and came almost running across the kitchen, face to face with me. 'You what did you say What was that? What did you say?' He grabbed my collar and put his fist close against my face.

'These melodramatics —— '

'Don't melodram me with your fancy talk!' I was seized, not with fear or anger but with sheer helplessness at the thought that these were beautiful Josiah Olroyd lines and I could not point them out to anybody, or even scoff.

'I merely said —— '

'Talk bloody properly! You were talking different a minute ago, weren't you? What did you just say to your grandma? What did you say?'

'Well don't pull him round, that shirt's clean on,' my mother said, anxiously.

'I'll clean shirt him! I'll clean shirt him round his bloody earhole! With his bloody fountain pens and his bloody suède shoes! Well he doesn't go out tonight! *I* know where he gets it from. He stops in tonight, and tomorrow night anall!'

I stood by the sink, looking weary, seeking some facial expression that was not outside the histrionic experience of the family. I searched for something to say that would not sound clever or impertinent. From the lounge I heard Gran muttering, 'Cheeky young devil!' but her voice sounded thick and strange.

'Look —— '

'Don't look me! With your look this and look that! And you get all them bloody papers and books and rubbish thrown out, anall! Before I chuck 'em out first, and you with 'em!'

The only way into the conversation was to counterfeit the old man's blunt and blunted way of talking. I set my lips into the same loose, flabby shape and said in the rough voice: 'What's up, they're not hurting you, are they?'

'No, and they're not bloody hurting you, eether,' the old man said, taking over, in his mind anyway, the role of family wit.

He went back across the kitchen and picked up the shelf where he had dropped it. I stood there straightening my tie, not speaking. My mother looked at me, her 'You've done it now' look. The old man turned back.

'Anyway, I've finished with him. He knows where his suitcase is. If he wants to go to London he can bloody well go!'

'Oh, but he's not!' my mother said sharply. She had been dithering for some time, wondering which side she was on, and now she came down on mine, or what she thought was mine.

'I've finished with him! He can go!'

'Oh, but he's not!'

'He's going. He's going out.' The idea was building up attractively in the old man's mind. 'He's going!'

'Oh, but he's not. Oh, but he's not. Oh, but he is not.'

'Look,' I said. 'Can I settle this —— '

This time the old man ignored me.

'It's ever since he left school, complaining about this and that and t' other. If it isn't his boiled eggs it's summat else. You have to get special bloody *wheat* flakes for him cos he's seen 'em on television. Well I've had enough. I've had enough. He can go.'

'Oh, but he's not! Now you just listen to me, Geoffrey. He's not old enough to go to London, or anywhere else. You said yourself. He doesn't think. He gets ideas into his head.'

'Well he's going, he can get *that* idea into his head.'

'Oh, but he is not. Not while *I'm* here.'

The old man's anger died down as quickly as it had flared up. 'He wants to get into t' bloody army, that's what he wants to do,' he said.

'Yes, and you want to get into t' bloody army as well,' my mother said.

This exchange of epigrams seemed to mark the end of the conversation. I turned to go.

'Where's he going *now*?' the old man said.

'I'm going to be sick,' I said viciously.

I went into the lounge, expecting Gran to toss her widow's mite into the controversy as I passed. I glanced at her as I walked towards the hall door, and saw at once, with a quick sense of panic, why she was so silent.

I shouted: 'Mother! Quick!' and looked up at the ceiling rather than at my grandmother. She was sitting in her arm-chair in a curiously rigid position, her yellow face convulsed, her neck ricked back. Specks of foam appeared on her lips and her watering eyes were bulging. She was trying to cry out, but no sounds came. Her skinny hands gripped the arms of her chair and her back was arched as though she had frozen in the act of getting up.

My mother and the old man came rushing into the room. 'Now look what you've done!' my mother cried. The old man dashed over to open the window.

He shouted: 'She's having a bloody fit, can't you see. Get t' smelling salts! Go on, then, frame yourself!'

Glad to get out of it, I galloped upstairs for the smelling salts. Gran's fits, occurring nowadays with increasing regularity, always filled me with dread and, I could not help it, disgust. I had a horror that I would one day be alone with her in the house when she threw one, and I was often haunted by the thought of what I would do in these circumstances. Rummaging around in my mother's dressing-table for the smelling salts, automatically conning the contents of the drawer to see if she had found anything of mine and hidden it, I realised that emerging from my panic was the old thought that perhaps this time Gran would die and there would be no more scenes. I tried to push the thought out by the counting and quoting method: Seventy-four, ninety-six, the Lord is my shepherd I shall not want. Calming a little, I no longer hoped that she was dead but that she was all right, or at least looking all right on the face of it, with the foam wiped off her lips and everything looking normal. I found the green bottle of smelling salts and went downstairs. At the turn of the stairs, scraping my shoe against the loose stair-rod, I told myself that I would count five and that at the end of that time she would have recovered, and I would go in.

I counted slowly, one, two, three, four, five, six. The hall door opened suddenly and the old man was peering round urgently. 'Come on, what you bloody doing?' I jumped the remaining stairs and handed him the bottle. 'Still feel sick,' I muttered. He shut the door in my face.

I walked slowly back upstairs, trying to *make* myself feel sick, but with no success. I went into my room and lay shivering on the bed. I strained my ears to listen for the voices downstairs, and told myself that I could hear the faint voice of Gran, and that that meant she was all right now. To get the incident out of my head I tried out a piece of No. 1 thinking, concerning my own death and the grief of the family. It tapered out and, feeling more at ease, I began to think aggressively, and then constructively, casting myself slowly into the role of master of the house. There was an insurance man bullying Gran into taking out a funeral policy, but she was too dim to know what it was all about. I came in just as the insurance man was becoming sneering and abusive. 'Would you mind, sir? This lady happens to be my grandmother.' – 'And who are you?' – 'Let us say that I have some experience in these matters.'

By now there were definitely voices downstairs, and I heard the old man going out into the garage. He wouldn't be going into the garage if everything were not all right. I breathed in deeply and began to sing quietly to myself. I rolled myself off the bed, stood around indecisively for a moment, then kneeled down and dragged the Guilt Chest out, checking the stamp edging only perfunctorily and not worrying overmuch whether they had been in it or not. It was time for another decision. I opened the wardrobe and got down the biggest sheet of brown paper I could find. I spread it out over the bed. Then I fell once again into a mild stupor, putting the recent conversation downstairs into some kind of glassy-eyed perspective. Brooding over Gran's complaint about my old raincoat in the bathroom, I remembered with a jolt the letter still there in it. I bounded into the bathroom and felt for it in my raincoat-cum-dressing-gown pocket. It was still there. I took it out and tried to remember the way I had folded it. They would surely have mentioned the matter if they had opened it and read it. I smoothed the letter out, and fluff fell out of the creases. I read it again.

Dear Mr Fisher,

Many thanks for script and gags, I can use some of the gags and pay accordingly. As for staff job, well, I regret to tell you, I do not have 'staff' beside my manager, but several of the boys do work for me, you might be interested in this. Why not call in for a chat next time you are in London? Best of luck and keep writing, Danny Boon.

Read in this light with the old man's threat to kick me out tentatively expressed it not actually confirmed, it did not seem after all much to go on. The thought of being in London began to fill me, once again, with apprehension. I walked back into the bedroom and took out the pound notes that I had been hoarding in my wallet. There were nine of them. I emptied my loose change out on to the sheet of wrapping paper on the bed: fourteen and sixpence. Nine pounds fourteen and sixpence. But I could not do the complicated sums of subtracting rail fare, rents, meals and the rest of it. I put the money away and turned back to the Guilt Chest.

Carefully, I winkled out a stack of about three dozen calendars and piled them on the sheet of brown paper. There seemed to be room for more. I got another dozen, and then wrapped the whole lot up, finding a length of string in the elephant-shaped vase on the bedroom mantelpiece. They made a heavy parcel, heavier than I had expected. I closed the Guilt Chest, putting the stamp-edging in a new position, and went downstairs, humping my parcel with me. In the hall I picked up a gramophone record that had been there for days, waiting to go back to the shop.

I went nervously into the lounge. Gran was sitting in her chair with a shawl over her shoulders, drinking weak tea and moaning composedly to show that she was still not herself. I breathed heavily with relief and went through into the kitchen, where my mother had started making scones.

'Is she all right?' I said gruffly.

'As all right as she'll ever be,' my mother said wearily, in her martyr's voice. I decided to let it go at that.

She nodded towards the parcel under my arm.

'What's that?'

'Books. Papers. Records,' I said.

'Where are you going with them?'

'Chucking them out, like he told me to,' I said, using my own martyr's voice.

'Don't be silly,' my mother said easily, and went on baking. I walked out of the house. The old man was still messing about in the garage.

Instead of walking down Cherry Row I walked up it, into Valley Gardens, along Valley Gardens into Moorside Gardens, and along Moorside Gardens past the builders' huts and over the rubbish tip that led steeply down into Stradhoughton Moor.

Stradhoughton Moor was a kind of pastoral slum on the edge of the town. It was fringed on Moorside by the dyeworks, Stradhoughton Town football ground and some public lavatories. The centre of the Moor was paved with cinders, where generations had tipped their slag and ashes, and where the annual fairs were held. There was a circumference of sparse yellow grass where the old men walked in summer, and I took the path they had worn towards a pocket of stone cottages, mostly condemned, that huddled miserably together in a corner of the Moor. Behind the cottages Stradhoughton Moor rose steeply again, out of an ashpit, to meet the scraggy allotments and, beyond them, the real moors of Houghtondale, such as were illustrated in the Council yearbook. I intended to drop my parcel of calendars down a pot-hole.

I enjoyed walking here. Given a quiet day I could always talk to myself, and it was easy to picture the cliff-like, craggy boundaries of the Moor as the borders of Ambrosia. The sun was still out, in a watery sort of way, and there was a hard, metal-grey shine on the afternoon. The faint waves of shouting, and all other noises, sounded remote and not very real, as though heard through a sheet of glass.

In Ambrosia, we were settling down to a shaky peace. The reactionary Dr Grover, weakened it was true by his Quisling record but still a power to be reckoned with, had got hold of some letters I had written to Arthur, outlining our plans for taking over the state. Liz, potentially the country's first home secretary, was abolishing the prisons.

I had reached the broken-down cottages by now. 'Mr President,' I said aloud, negotiating the ashpit and wondering whether to drop the parcel of calendars in it to be found, soggy and disintegrating, like a baby's body in a shoe box, 'Democracy is a stranger to Ambrosia. And yet this is a country of democrats. You know what this is?' – I held up the gramophone record I had brought out with me – 'It is a ballot paper. Mr President, I will not rest until we have democracy *by vote* in this, er, ancient land of ours.'

I scrambled up the ashpit until I had reached the top of the Moor and was standing on the verge of grass surrounding the allotments. I looked down over the acre of cinders, across the lines of washing and the terrace-end pubs, the grandstand roof of the football ground advertising Bile Beans, and the black stone police station.

'We will rebuild ——' I began in the ringing voice. I heard a slight crunching noise behind me, and turned round. A rough path of stone chippings led through the plots of beet-root and big blue cabbages towards the tufty moorland. Staggering along the path like some lost shepherd, doubtless living out his own private dreams as Dr Johnson or George Borrow or somebody, came Councillor Duxbury himself, dabbing his streaming eyes and clutching his gnarled old stick.

My heart missed a beat, and I wondered quickly how many beats it had missed this day, and whether it could only miss so many before you were dead, and if so how far I was off the total. There was nothing to dodge behind, unless I cared to jump back into the ashpit, but in any case he had seen me. I composed my face to look as though I wasn't doing anything, and tightened my grip on the suddenly enormous parcel of calendars under my arm.

Councillor Duxbury came flapping down the stone path, raising his stick in salute.

'Afternoon, lad!' he called in his rich, so-called Yorkshire relish voice.

'Afternoon, Councillor!' I called in the robust voice.

'It's a sunny 'un, this! 'Appen tha's watching t' football?'

'Nay, ahm' just bahn for a walk ower t' moor.' I always talked to Councillor Duxbury in his own dialect, half-mockingly, half-compulsively, usually goading myself into internal hysterics when I thought how I would reproduce the conversation to Arthur later.

'What's ta got theer, then? T' crown jewels?' He pointed with his stick at my parcel, his old face set in the serious, deadpan expression that had won him his tiresome reputation as a wag in the council chamber.

'Nay, old gramophone records,' I said, wildly producing the one record I did have, as proof. He did not ask me where I was taking them.

'Aye, ther' were nowt like that,' he said. His memory had been jogged so many times by *Echo* interviewers that he now regarded every statement as a cue for his reminiscences, and no longer bothered to add 'when I were a lad' or 'fot'ty year ago.' 'Ther' were nowt like that. We had to make our own music if we wanted it, else go without.' He rattled on as though he were himself an old gramophone that has just been kicked back into action. I was not sure that he knew who I was. Entirely lost in himself he began to mumble about the Messiah and I let him, full of frothy self-congratulation because I would be one up on Arthur when the next Duxbury routine came up.

'No, ther' were nowt like that.' He stopped at last to wipe his nose, making a ritual of it with a coloured handkerchief about the size of a bed-sheet. He paused between sniffs and shot me what he imagined to be a playful glance, the expression he always wore when he asked people how old they thought he was.

'Does ta think ah could climb down yon ashpit?'

'Nay, tha'd break thi neck, Councillor!' I said, giving him entirely the wrong answer. He gave me a sour look and said: 'Aye, well ah'sll have to manage it, whether or no. Ah'm bahn down to t' police station.'

My heart missed another beat, or rather ceased operating altogether for a second.

'What's ta bahn down theer for, then?' I told myself optimistically that if it were about me he would be going to the town hall, never mind the local police station. Besides, he didn't know who I was.

Councillor Duxbury chuckled. 'We're pulling't down.'

I gulped with relief, although my heart was still at it. 'Tha's not, is ta?' I said, packing some incredulity into my voice.

'Aye, we are that. All yon cottages anall, they're going. And they won't get *council* houses for three and six a week, neether.'

I shook my head in sympathy, and saw that he was going into another of his reveries. I transferred my parcel from one arm to the other.

'It's all change,' said Councillor Duxbury. 'All change, nowadays. T' old buildings is going. T' old street is going. T' trams, they've gone.'

'Aye,' I said, sighing with him. 'It's not t' same wi' t' buses, is it?' One good shove, I thought, and he would be down at the bottom of the ashpit, where he wanted to be.

'It were all horse-drawn trams, and afore that we had to walk. It's all change. T' old mills is going. T' old dialect, *that's* going,' he said. I suddenly realised that he knew perfectly well that I did not talk in dialect all the time, and also that it was ridiculous to imagine that he did not know I worked for him. To prevent him saying whatever he might have been going to say next, I began to talk, looking desperately down over Stradhoughton Moor.

'Well, progress is all very well,' I said. 'But it's a pity we don't have a Yorkshire tradition o' progress.' I was trying to modify the dialect so that I could drop out of it completely within the minute. I nodded down at the police station. 'I don't mind dark satanic mills, but by gum when it comes to dark satanic shops, dark satanic housing estates and dark satanic police stations —— ' I broke off, realising that I had never worked out the end of this sentence. I looked at Councillor Duxbury for the feedline but he was away, staring glassily over the Moor.

'– that's different,' I concluded lamely. He did not seem inclined to speak. 'And yet,' I went on, grabbing half-remembered tufts of my Man o' the Dales conversation, 'and yet we've got to remember, this isn't a religion, it's a county. We've, er —— '

I tailed off again. Councillor Duxbury had the fixed expression that old men have when they are lost in their thoughts, or what they claim are their thoughts, not listening to a word I was saying. A quick gust of wind swept around our ankles. I opened my mouth to speak again, remembering another bit, and then suddenly, without moving, he carved straight into my monologue.

'Tha's a reet one wi' them calendars, i'n't ta?'

I blanched, rocked on my heels and nearly fell over the grass edge into the ashpit below. I looked into his face to see if there was any suspicion of a boys-will-be-boys chuckle but he maintained his deadpan look as though he were telling wry jokes at a masonic dinner.

'By, tha's capped me theer, Councillor!' was all I could think of to say.

'Aye, and tha's capped me anall! Ah were reet taken back when Shadrack rang me up on t' telephone. Ah'd ha' thowt a lad like thee would have had more sense.' He spoke easily and not sternly, like a Yorkshire butler filling in plot-lines in a dialect comedy. I fancied that he was peering with keen suspicion at the parcel of calendars, and wondered if it were true that there were wise old men and he was one of them. I didn't know what to make of it. Even if he knew I worked for him, I was surprised that he could distinguish me from Stamp and Arthur. I had a reckless impulse to tell him that I *was* Arthur and that he was getting the two of us mixed up.

I said nothing.

'So tha's going to London, is ta?' he said with mild interest, as though the subject of the calendars had been settled entirely to his satisfaction.

Hopefully, I said: 'Aye, ah'm just about thraiped wi' Stradhoughton.' I remembered too late that 'thraiped' was a word Arthur and I had made up.

'How does ta mean?'

'It's neither muckling nor mickling,' I said, using another invented phrase in my complete panic.

'Aye.' The old man poked the ground with his stick, and said again, 'Aye.' I had no indication what he was thinking about at all. I tried hard to keep talking, but I could not think of a single word of any description.

'Well tha's gotten me in a very difficult position,' he said weightily, at last.

'How does ta mean, Councillor?'

He studied me keenly, and I realised for the first time, with a sinking heart, that he was not as daft as he looked.

'Is ta taking a rise out o' me, young man?'

I felt myself flushing, and found my whole personality shifting into the familiar position of sheepishness and guilt. 'No, of course not.'

'Well just talk as thi mother and father brought thee up to talk then. Ah've had no education, ah had to educate myself, but that's no reason for thee to copy t' way *I* talk.' He spoke sharply but kindly, in a voice of authority with some kind of infinite wisdom behind it, and at that moment I felt genuinely ashamed.

'Now sither. We'll noan go ower t' ins and outs of it, tha's been ower all that down at t' office. But young Shadrack theer thinks ah ought to have a word wi' thi' father about thee. What does ta say to that?'

'I don't know,' I muttered, hanging my head. I wondered how I could ask him, without actually begging for mercy, not to talk to the old man.

'Well don't look as if tha's lost a bob and fun sixpence! Tha's not deead yet!'

I looked up at him and gave him a thin, grateful smile.

'Straighten thi back up! That's better. Now sither. Ah don't know what ah'sll do. Ah'sll have to think about what's best. But sither —— ' He gripped my arm. I did not feel embarrassed; I was able, even, to look steadily into his eyes. 'Sither. Tha'rt a young man. Tha' got a long way to go. But tha can't do it by thisen. Now think on.'

He released my arm, leaving me feeling that he had said something sage and shrewd, although I was unable to fathom quite what he was getting at. He was stuffing his handkerchief into his overcoat pocket, preparing to go. I did not want him to go. I did not feel afraid. I felt a kind of tentative serenity and I wanted him to go on with his old man's advice, telling me the things I should do.

'My grandma's poorly,' I said suddenly, without even knowing that I was talking. But he did not seem to hear.

'Ah'm glad to have had t' chance o' talking to thee,' he said. He turned and began to make his way gingerly down the gentlest slope of the ashpit, feeling the way with his shiny stick. Half-way down he turned back awkwardly. 'Think on,' he said.

I looked down after him, only just beginning to realise that for the first time I wanted to tell somebody about it, and that I could very probably have explained it all to him. I had to resist an impulse to call back after him.

I stood there until he was safely on the grass perimeter surrounding the stretch of cinders. I had a feeling, one that I wanted to keep. It was a feeling of peace and melancholy. I was not at all afraid. I walked happily along the rough stone path through the allotments to the quiet moorland beyond, and even while I was burying the calendars the feeling was still with me.

Chapter Seven

The Witch was already fishing in her handbag for an orange, but I was in a rare mood of optimism, as though I were starting a new life or something. We were on top of the No. 17 bus, bound for the Corporation Cemetery. I was humming quietly, and fingering two or three of Stamp's passion pills in my pocket. The Witch was fuming to herself over the approaches that had been made to her by various men in raincoats while she waited for me in St Botolph's Passage. Luckily for me the experience had put her out of mood for window-shopping.

Half-way to the cemetery, she was still going on about it. 'There *are* some nasty people about.'

'Mm,' I said. 'Have a passion pill.' I held two of the little black beads out in the palm of my hand. 'Energy tablets, they are,' I added hastily, realising what I had just said. 'We always call them passion pills. They're supposed to give you energy.'

The Witch was digging her thumb-nail viciously into the peel of her orange. The bus was passing a row of advertising hoardings.

'Look, there y'are,' I cried excitedly, clutching her sleeve and jabbing at the window. '*Too* late. It was an advert for them. P.P., they're called. That's why they're nicknamed passion pills. You're supposed to take two.'

The Witch, stuffing bits of orange into her mouth, gave me her pitying look. 'What *is* the boy talking about?' she said.

I put on the frank and open grin and held out the two black pills. 'Very nice with fruit!' I said in the persuasive voice.

The Witch made some heavy weather over a sigh. 'Better humour the boy,' she said with an attempt at mock-resignation. She took the two pills in her mouth and knocked them back with a slice of orange. 'Satisfied?'

I sat back contentedly and lit a cigarette.

'Fifth today.'

'Last one,' the Witch cautioned.

Life seemed temporarily good. We got off the bus at the cemetery gates and walked up the broad red-gravel avenue between the white gravestones. Sometimes, in expansive moments such as this, I could understand what the Witch found so fascinating about this place. In fact it sometimes fascinated *me.* It was open, tidy and secure, like the campus in an American college musical. After the black, streaky tombs of St Botolph's churchyard there was something pleasantly normal about the symmetrical rows of neat headstones and the tidy oblongs of clean pebbles. All the people here seemed to have died a modern, healthy sort of death.

We strolled on to the grass verge between the graves, making our way to the public shelter outside the red brick chapel at the end of the long drive. The Witch, completely in her element, darted busily from one grave to another, admiring the angels and the September flowers, and crying 'Oh, look, pet, isn't it *sweet!*' whenever she found a stone crib. From time to time she would stoop reverently over a headstone and read out one of the verses chipped in gold, square lettering.

With you dearest Mother and darling dad,
Happy were the years we had,
And it is comfort in our pain
You are now together again

I listened to all this benevolently. So far as I was concerned, this was the scene when you see a close-up of a clock and the minute hand moves round a quarter of an hour to show the passage of time. Remembering the fiasco earlier in the day, I decided to give her a good twenty-five minutes this time, and she had quoted enough verses to fill an anthology before we reached the deserted shelter by the mock-Norman door of the burial chapel.

I got her snuggling up to me in the dark corner where we had carved our initials; that was the first step.

'Happy?'

'Mmmmm.'

I kissed her. She responded drowsily.

'Barbara? Tell me, how do you feel?'

'Contented,' she said, squeezing up to me kittenishly.

'You don't feel – you know, restless?'

'No.'

I sat there stroking her sleeve, trying to get some action out of her. I put my mouth close to hers again, but she was messing about making little kissing noises with her lips, and it was impossible to get at her for any length of time.

'Would you like another energy tablet?'

'No thank you, pet. They seem to make me sleepy.'

I grabbed hold of her arms roughly and urgently. She sat up, recognising the signs.

'Barbara,' I said in the pleading voice. 'Barbara!'

'Don't be angry again, pet,' she pleaded, clutching her handbag full of oranges in alarm.

'I'm not angry, just sad. Barbara – you know you're making me ill, don't you?'

'Poor Billy! Why am I making you ill?'

'Dalling! Have you ever heard of repressions? The nervous reactions that affect men who aren't, well —— ' The only ending I could think of for the sentence was a phrase of Stamp's, 'Getting it regular.' I let the thing peter out.

'I know what you mean, pet,' the Witch said, gently but desperately, as though she were soothing a dangerous lunatic. 'But we must be patient. We must. We'd only regret it.' But I was already regretting it. I found myself, quite suddenly, not caring a damn one way or the other, only wondering what I was doing here in a cemetery with a stone woman, anyway.

I muttered 'Forget it' and leaned back in the hard wooden shelter with my eyes closed, calculating how soon I could get away. I had been meaning to scheme out some way of keeping the Witch out of the Roxy tonight, out of the way of Rita, and I decided that it was high time I got to work on it. A tentative plot began to form in my mind; arranging to meet the Witch outside the Odeon, not turning up, and then explaining the whole unfortunate misunderstanding when she came to tea tomorrow. A warning bell sounded in my brain on the idea of the Witch coming to tea. *See Witch re Captain.* The words I had scribbled down hours before suddenly flashed like a neon sign in my head. I sat up again, sharply.

'Dalling!'

'Mmmm?' She was almost asleep.

'Dalling, are you still coming to tea tomorrow?'

The Witch sat up herself and shot me a keen glance, daring me to wriggle out of it.

'Of course. That's why I was hoping you would have got my engagement ring back.'

'Good.'

I swallowed. I had rehearsed this once, but that was days ago. I tried to visualise the stage instructions, looking studiously down at the stone-flagged floor and tracing one of the cracks with my foot.

'There's something I want to tell you,' I said in the low voice.

The Witch said nothing but, employing her main defence mechanism, stiffened.

'You know what you were saying about loving me even if I were a criminal?'

'Well?' in her icy voice. We had had a fairly tortured evening once when the Witch had cornered me into admitting that I would love her in every conceivable circumstance – age, infirmity, unfaithfulness (the idea of her being unfaithful had rather charmed me) and criminal record being taken into account. I had had no option but to fire the same litany back at her, and had got so far as to make her agree that even if I shot her father and mother she would still, she thought, love me.

'I wonder if you'll still love me when you've heard what I've got to say,' I said.

The Witch was rapidly withdrawing into a cocoon of formality.

'You see – well, you know that I've got a fairly vivid imagination, don't you?'

'Well you have to have, if you're going to be a scriptwriter, don't you?' she said smugly. There were occasions when I would have willingly shot *her*, never mind her relations.

'Well *be*ing a script-writer,' I continued ponderously, 'I'm perhaps a bit inclined to let my imagination run away with me. As you know.'

The Witch said nothing, but she was beginning to breathe heavily through her nostrils.

'You see, if – if we're going to have our life together, and the cottage, and little Billy and little Barbara and the wishing-well and all that, there's some things we've got to get cleared up.' I nearly added 'and implemented'.

'What things?'

According to my stage instructions I was to give her a frank, honest glance. I was unable to do it, and decided to rely on a frank, honest profile.

'Some of the things I'm afraid I've been telling you.'

The Witch said, in her direct, devastating way: 'Do you mean you've been telling *lies*?'

'Well not lies exactly, but I suppose I've been – well, exaggerating some things. Being a script writer . . .' Another idea crossed my mind, that of slapping the Witch across the mouth and striding out of the cemetery, never to meet her again. I put it away. 'Well, for instance, there's that business about my father. Him being a sea captain.'

In a weak moment, or rather in a panoramic series of weak moments, I had told the Witch that during the war the old man had been the captain of a destroyer. He had been partly responsible for sinking the *Graf Spee* before being captured – one of the first men to be captured by U-boats, as a matter of fact – and had spent three years in a prisoner-of-war camp. He had been wounded in the leg, which still gave him some trouble.

'You mean he wasn't a sea captain, I suppose?' said the Witch, and I was surprised that *she* didn't seem surprised.

'He wasn't even in the navy,' I said.

'And what about him being a prisoner-of-war? Don't say *that* was all lies.'

'Yes.'

The Witch turned away with a quick movement of the head, bringing tears to her eyes without difficulty. I suspected that she had perfected the whole action in front of a mirror. Its point was to make it quite evident that she was turning away and not just looking away. Reaching out for the most banal remark I could find, I said:

'Are you cross?'

There was a practised silence. The Witch gave it thirty seconds and then said:

'No, I'm not cross. Just disap*poi*nted, that's all. It sounds as though you were *ashamed* of your father.'

I sat bold upright and steamed the heat into my voice. 'I'm *not* ashamed, I'm not, I'm not!'

'Otherwise why say he was a sea captain – ? What was he?'

I had to stop myself from saying 'A conscientious objector'

and starting the whole thing over again. I said: 'He wasn't anything. He wasn't fit. He has trouble with his knee.'

'The knee he's supposed to have been shot in, I suppose.'

'Yes,' and I was now talking belligerently. 'Another thing, we haven't got a budgie.'

I had told her that we kept a yellow budgerigar called Roger. I had regularly given her communiques about its antics and there had been a highlight when Roger had flown out of his cage and nearly been caught by Sarah, the tabby.

'Or a cat,' I said.

The Witch was shuffling her handbag about and buttoning her coat to give the impression that she was about to leave.

'How many other lies have you been telling me?'

'My sister.' The Witch had roughly the same story about my imaginary sister as I had given to Arthur's mother.

'Don't tell me you haven't got a *sis*ter.'

'I did have, but she's dead.' This time it was out before I could prevent it. I ran rapidly over this new turn, and within seconds I had established death from tuberculosis, and a quiet funeral. 'If you still want to come tomorrow, they never talk about her,' I said.

'I'm not sure I *shall* be coming, now,' said the Witch. She shuddered elaborately. 'I've always hated – lying.'

A happy thought struck me. In my pocket I still had the miniature silver cross that had spilled out of her handbag in St Botolph's churchyard – the one she was supposed to have given back to her cousin Alec.

'Have you?' I said. I decided against producing the thing triumphantly and waving it under her nose, for the moment at least. I went into the hard voice and said: 'Look, Barbara, we all have our faults. I have mine. You have yours.'

'I don't tell *lies*,' said the Witch.

'Don't you?'

'No!'

'What about that cross or whatever it was that you were supposed to have given back to your cousin?'

'Well, I *did* give it back,' said the Witch. I was satisfied to see the same smooth expression on her face that I wore so regularly myself.

'Did you?' I said cryptically. She looked down at her handbag and back at me.

'I told you I'd given it back and I *gave* it back.'

'All right.' I stood up as though washing my hands of the whole business. From the hard voice into the matter-of-fact voice. 'Look. I've got to go into town now. You probably won't believe anything I say after this, but I may as well tell you that I've been offered a job in London. It depends on your attitude whether I take it or not.'

The Witch got to her feet, contriving a dazed expression. I felt like gripping her by the lapels of her coat and saying coarsely: 'Look, chum, I do all these tricks myself. I *know* them. Pack it in.'

'I shall never know whether you're telling the truth after this,' she said. She walked with me down the gravel drive towards the cemetery gates, almost falling over her own feet in her attempts to look straight in front of her.

As we were passing the last grave I said in the bitter voice: 'Well I know what *my* epitaph will be.'

She did not reply at first, so I let her wait for it. At length she said: 'What?' reluctantly.

'"Here lies Billy Fisher,"' I said.

I put just the right amount of ruefulness in my voice, and it took effect. She caught my hand impulsively and said: 'Don't be cross with yourself.'

At the cemetery gates she stopped and held my hands at arm's length, as though for inspection, 'Billy?'

'Yes, dalling?'

'Promise me something?'

'That I'll never lie to you again?' She nodded. 'I'll never lie to you again,' I said.

Holding hands, we walked out of the cemetery. The first person I saw, coming towards us and too near for me to do anything about it, was Arthur's mother, carrying a bunch of pansies.

Out of the side of my mouth I said rapidly: 'Do as I say, I'll explain later!' As Arthur's mother came alongside us, I smiled broadly.

'Hullo, Mrs Crabtree. I don't think you've met my sister. Sheila, this is Mrs Crabtree.'

Arthur's mother looked at me as though I had hit her. It suddenly struck me that I had made the wrong decision. She said indignantly:

'I'm afraid you've picked the wrong person to play your tricks with *this* time. I happen to know Barbara very well.'

The Witch, for public consumption only, gave me her tolerant, more-in-sorrow look.

'I think it's his queer sense of humour,' she said.

'Got to catch a tram,' I gabbled. 'Bus.' A No. 17 was pulling slowly away from the bus stop. I jumped on and galloped up the stairs, getting the Ambrosian repeater gun into position.

Chapter Eight

'What, is *this* for me as well?' asked Rita incredulously.

I nodded, my mouth so full of egg sandwich that my eyes were watering. 'Been robbing a bank,' I chuntered, spluttering food. It was already five o'clock, and the first time I had eaten since breakfast.

'Cugh! Got owt else you don't want?' She was genuinely delighted, more pleased, in fact, than she had been over the engagement ring. She put the silver cross round her neck, fumbling under the metallic blonde hair to fasten the slender chain.

'Joan of Arc,' said Arthur.

'Oo, it's woke up again!' She bared her teeth at him, registering exaggerated scorn. Afraid that she had perhaps been sounding too grateful and had made a fool of herself, she said dubiously, peering down at the cross: 'Aren't you supposed to go to church or summat when you wear one of these?'

Arthur said: 'Yes, you've got to take a vow of chastity.'

'Get back in the knifebox, bighead!' Rita picked up my empty plate, a move I recognised as an obscure gesture of affection. 'You can bring me a fur coat tomorrer,' she said genially. She went back to the counter, leaving us sitting at the rockety table in the corner of the Kit-Kat by the huge, throbbing refrigerator.

'The sexfulness is terrific,' Arthur said, watching her go.

I was back in the buoyant, almost hysterical mood.

'Lo, she is the handmaiden of my desires!' I said, raising a solemn right hand. Arthur took the cue to go into the Bible routine.

'And a voice spake,' he said in a loud, quavering voice. 'And the voice said Lo, who was that lady I saw ye with last cock-crow?'

'And Moses girded up his loins and said Verily, that was no lady, that was my spouse,' I responded.

'Yea, and it was so.'

'Yea, even unto the fifth and sixth generations.'

We finished our coffee and got up, guffawing and blowing kisses at Rita. 'Don't do owt I wouldn't do!' she called, in an unusual mood herself.

We left the glass doors wide open, the doughnut-eaters yelling 'Door!' after us, and walked out into Moorgate and across the road towards Town Arcade.

I had got over the feeling of guilt at meeting Arthur so soon after the hideous contretemps with his mother. I had been thinking of telling him about it, in one form or another, but now I was glad that I hadn't.

We walked into Town Arcade shouting: 'Paymer! Paymer! War declared! Paymer!' and our voices echoed under the arched glass roof. The women shoppers, shuffling miserably after each other with their string bags and their packets of cream biscuits, stared at us. 'Paymer, lady?' I called, flourishing an imaginary *Echo*. To my own surprise, I found that I was still carrying under my arm the gramophone record I had taken out of the house hours ago.

'Let's go take the mickey out of Maurie,' I said.

Maurie was the owner of the X-L Disc Bar at the top of the Arcade, a slight, dapper little man who looked like an Armenian. He was interested in youth work and all the rest of it, and was always going on about showing tolerance and treating everybody as adults. When we had nothing to do we would go in and bully him. 'Hey, Maurie, this record's got all grooves in it.'

'Wonder if we'll get any buckshee records out of him?' said Arthur. We opened the door with our feet and almost fell into the shop.

On Saturday afternoons the X-L Disc Bar was crowded with girls in gipsy ear-rings and youths in drainpipe trousers. They were the same people that we saw in the Roxy every week, but we never saw them anywhere else in Stradhoughton. They seemed to be transported invisibly from one place to another. They made me feel curiously old-fashioned in my stained raincoat and my crumpled suit, and I put on the intellectual act, sloping one shoulder down and trying to look as though the record under my arm was a copy of *Under Milk Wood*. One of the Kit-Kat crowd, doing a sort of skaters' waltz round the shop, called 'Rag-bones!' but nobody else took any notice.

The Disc Bar would not have made a good subject for Man o' the Dales' Yorkshire Sketchbook. It had been a quite passably modern record shop when Maurie first opened it, but under his policy of live and let live it had been quickly reduced to a glass shambles. The cone-shaped ashtray stands, their bright yellow smudged with black, were already tilted, broken and abandoned. The showcases, which were supposed to hang in mid-air on steel wires, sagged and lurched so dangerously that they had to be propped up on old packing cases. One of them was broken, a great jagged crack going along one corner. There were scuff marks all along the orange walls.

The girls in their tartan trousers swarmed around the record booths, leaving the doors swinging open untidily, so that half a dozen melodies – the pop songs, the trumpet specialities and the jazzed-up hymns – met and collided somewhere in the middle of the shop. A boy of about sixteen in a leather lumber jacket was leaning against the counter, juggling with a plastic record sleeve. Little Maurie, in his red braces, was trying to make himself heard. 'Would you mind? I know it's a great temptation, but would you mind?'

Arthur pirouetted across the shop like a dancer, using the peculiar gliding steps that seemed to be more or less obligatory in this centre. He found a cluster of friends from the band that played at the Roxy, and was immediately swallowed up with them in the corner. I stood by myself, hesitating. The odd thing was that he seemed to know everybody and I didn't. In the No. 1 thinking it was sometimes the other way round.

I heard a familiar, grating voice behind me and looked round. It was Stamp, holding up an L.P. and shouting: 'Hey, Maurie, is this a record?' – a joke, if you could call it a joke, that he had used a hundred times before. Stamp was never out of the Disc Bar. Little Maurie was the leader of the youth club whose illiterate posters Stamps was always designing. 'Hey, Maurie! Maurie! Is this a record?' I cuffed his arm so that he almost dropped the L.P. 'No, slipped disc,' I said.

'Oh, they've let *you* out, have they?' jeered Stamp, his eyes narrowing maliciously.

'Yes, they wanted to make room for you,' I said. I was glad

to have met even Stamp. I turned away, looking around the shop to see if there was anybody else I knew.

'I say!' Stamp called me back.

'I wouldn't come in on Monday if I were you,' he said.

'I wouldn't come in on *Tuesday* if I were you. Why not?'

He was grinning in the malevolent way he had when he had got hold of a piece of rich bad news. 'I've just been back to the office to get some stuff,' he said. 'Shadrack's adding up your postage book.'

'After you with Shadrack,' I said. I suddenly felt ill. In the light voice: 'Did he say anything?'

'What?'

'Did he *say* anything, dozey! About the stinking postage book?'

'No, he was just muttering to himself. He had all the money and all the stamps out, though. He was adding it all up. How much have you knocked off?'

'Haven't knocked anything off.' Some of Stamp's friends were hovering round, staring at me. 'Only the book's not up to date, that's all,' I said.

'Borstal here we come,' said Stamp. He turned back to his friends, tittering. Over his shoulder, he said casually: 'Your mate's upstairs.'

I knew at once, with a quick vibration running through me, whom he was talking about, exactly as I had known when he mentioned her this morning. I glanced involuntarily up the stairs where the classical department was, all thought of Shadrack going out of my head before it had time even to take root. One of Stamp's friends, a dopey-looking youth in an Italian striped suit, said: *'Git in there, Charlie!'* I walked slowly up the stairs, the noise fading into a cacophonous backwash. Things I had forgotten came back and I was already steeped in the familiar atmosphere, the sense of freshness, relief, absurd comfort, anticipation, and the hint of some elusive scent that I knew for a fact did not exist. I was already telling her, 'I could remember how you *smelled*, even!' The last thing I heard was Stamp shouting, away in the distance, down in the shop, 'Hey, Maurie, this record's got a hole in it!'

The classical department, usually deserted on a Saturday afternoon, had an almost public library air about it. It was thickly carpeted, with a single glass counter and a row of grey record booths. The rest of it was empty and light and spacious, and quiet. Liz was standing behind the counter, handing a record album to a middle-aged man in a black overcoat. She was talking to him in her comfortable, plummy voice. I knew that she had seen me out of the corner of her eye, and was putting the moment off, the same as I was.

I was trying on expressions, as though I carried a mirror about with me and was pulling faces in it. I tried to look stunned, because after all there was the material for it, and I tried to assemble some kind of definite emotion that I wasn't putting on or concocting out of the ingredients of the atmosphere she carried around with her. I found that what I had was a sensation of singing.

The man picked up the record album and went into one of the record booths, closing the door behind him.

I walked slowly forward to the counter.

'Hullo, Liz.'

'Hullo, Billy.'

I spoke in what I hoped was the low, husky voice, indicating the end of a long journey or something, but she spoke frankly and happily, as though she were delighted to see me and had no reason to hide what she felt.

We grinned at each other, full of relief, like people who have found each other again in a crowd. She was still wearing the same old things, the green suède jacket and the crumpled black skirt. But the crisp white blouse went well with her round, shiny face, the mousy hair and the eyes that laughed aloud.

'It's been a long time,' I said, knowing it was a cliché, in fact selecting it *as* a cliché, but trying to put some meaning into what I was saying.

She shook her head from side to side, happily, considering the point.

'Oh – a month. Five weeks.'

'I ought to say it seemed like years.'

She grinned again. Liz was the only girl I had ever met who knew *how* to grin, or anything about it. 'Isn't this *grand*?' she said.

'I could even remember how you smelled,' I said.

She gave me a mock bow. 'Thank you, kind sir, she said.'

'When did you get back?'

'Yesterday.'

'Thank you very much for ringing me up and telling me.'

She wrinkled her nose, not in the same way as the Witch but in a friendly, candid way. Liz never gave excuses.

'I would have seen you tonight, anyway,' she said. 'Are you going to the Roxy?'

Who isn't? I thought. I started rapidly disposing of personnel. The Witch, for one, would quite obviously be going into a nunnery or somewhere after this afternoon's business. Rita, if I stood her up, would not dream of paying her own way into the Roxy. I did not care, anyway, knowing that I could tell Liz all about it if I wanted to.

'Yes,' I said. 'But I wish you'd rung me up.'

'I hadn't time.' She grinned broadly again, telling me not to believe her and not to worry because it didn't matter, and it didn't. 'Ask me what I'm doing *here*.'

'What are you doing here?'

'Helping Maurie out for the day.' No time to ring me up, but time to help Maurie out. It still didn't matter. The only thing that crossed my mind was the vague question of how Liz knew Maurie. She seemed to know everybody. It was part of the enigma, one of the things about her that I could never get into the test-tube and examine.

'Well what have you been *do*ing all these weeks?' she said, bubbling over with it all. 'How's the script-writing? How are the songs? How's Arthur?' She was the only girl I knew who cared, or who could talk about things as though they really mattered. We began chattering, eagerly interrupting, laughing, grinning at each other as though we knew the whole joke about the world and understood it. We talked until the man in the record booth, whom we had both forgotten, emerged with the record album and paid for it and went away. It was nearly closing time.

'Ask me where I've been all these weeks,' said Liz.

'No,' I said steadily, not laughing this time. It was the one standing challenge between us and I had always told myself that I would never ask. I did not know any longer whether I was afraid to, or whether it was out of some kind of respect for her, or whether it was just an obsession like growing my thumb-nail until it was a quarter of an inch long.

'But you might have sent me a postcard,' I said.

'Postcards next time. If there is a next time,' she added softly.

I went downstairs again, waving to her. The crowd had thinned out, leaving a litter of discarded records and cigarette packets on the floor and on the glass showcases. Arthur had gone, and so had his friends from the band. Most of Stamp's crowd had gone too, but Stamp was still there, sniggering with Maurie at the counter.

The old gramophone record still under my arm, I remembered what I had come into the Disc Bar for in the first place. I was loth to approach Maurie without Arthur to back me up, but I decided to do so for Stamp's benefit.

'Hey, Maurie!' I said. 'Can I have the money back on this record?'

He glared at me, a sour look that was unusual for him, and snapped: 'Why?'

'It only *plays* one tune.'

Maurie rang open his cash register. 'Yes, I've been *watch*ing you,' he said venomously. 'I've been *hear*ing about you.' Stamp was leaning on the counter, trying to look as though he didn't know what was going on. 'You're another of these who come in here, thinking you own the shop. Well *I* don't know where you get your money from.'

Maurie always dribbled when he spoke. He sucked in vigorously with his upper lip, retrieving the thin spittle that had been trickling down his chin.

'Well we're having a big clear-out. From now on it's a shop, not a market-place. Take the money and clear out.'

He flung some coins on the scratched glass counter. I had to scrabble at them to pick them up. Stamp was finding it difficult not to break out sniggering again.

'And don't come back again!' said Maurie.

But I was whistling as I walked out of the shop, and I whistled all the way down the Arcade.

Chapter Nine

I did nothing but walk around town for an hour and a half, watching Saturday evening begin to happen and the slow queues forming outside the Odeon and the Gaumont. The people walked about as though they were really going somewhere. I stood for a quarter of an hour at the time, watching them get off the buses and disperse themselves about the streets. I was amazed and intrigued that they should all be content to be nobody but themselves.

When it was half-past seven I got on a bus myself, on my way to the New House, the pub where I did my club turn. As a rule I could not face this experience without a stiff shot of No. 1 thinking, seeing myself returning to Stradhoughton as the world-famous comedian, doing charity concerts and never losing the common touch. But tonight I did not think about it at all. When Liz was in Stradhoughton I could transport myself from hour to hour like a levitationist, so that all events between one meeting and another were things that happened to other people and not to me.

It was only when I got off the bus at Clogiron Lane and the New House was in sight that I began to unload the ballast and I was left, as usual, with nothing but a kind of desperate inertia.

The New House was an enormous drinking barracks that had been built to serve Cherry Row and the streets around it. The New House was not its proper title. According to the floodlit inn-sign stuck on a post in the middle of the empty car park, the pub was called the Who'd A Thought It. There had been a lot of droll speculation in Man o' the Dales' column about how this name had come about, but whatever the legend was it had fallen completely flat in Clogiron Lane. Nobody ever called the pub anything but the New House.

There was a windy, rubber-tiled hallway where the children squatted, eating potato crisps and waiting for their mothers. Two frosted-glass doors, embossed with the brewery trademark, led off it, one into the public bar and one into the saloon. It was necessary to take one route or the other to get into the concert-room; the only other alternative was to approach the concert-room direct through its own entrance and run the gauntlet of fat women, sitting in rows with their legs apart, shrieking with laughter and gulping down gin and orange. Either that or climb in through the lavatory window.

I decided on the public bar route. I smoothed my hair back, straightened my tie, and went in. I preferred the public bar, anyway. The men who sat here were refugees from the warm terrace-end pubs that had been pulled down; they sat around drinking mild and calling to each other across the room as though nothing had changed. 'Have you got them theer, Charlie?' – 'Aye, they're up in our garridge.' – 'I'll come down for 'em tomorrow morning.' They seemed to have secrets between them, and they reunited into a world of their own wherever they went. The few items in the New House that gave it anything like the feel of a pub – the dartboard, the cribbage markers, the scratched blind-box and the pokerwork sign that said IYBMADIBYO, if you buy me a drink I'll buy you one – were all part of the same portable world, as if they had been wheeled here in prams in the flight from the old things.

Through the smoke, a voice croaked jubilantly: 'Here he is – *the boy*!' and I realised at once that I had made another mistake. From this point I had to walk through a barricade of Formica-topped tables where all these men sat clacking dominoes and making their observations. I waved my hand flaccidly at one or two of the people I recognised. A man called Freddy Platt, who never did anything else but sit around drinking beer all day, started up.

'Nah lad, Billy! Where's thi dog?' The others laughed, and he looked around eagerly for someone to egg him on. 'He's forgotten t' dog ageean! Ask him what he's done wi' t' dog, Sam!'

'Where's thi dog, Billy?'

Once, in some kind of effort to prise myself into this community of theirs, where they were always selling each other things and sharing the same interests, I had asked Freddy Platt if he wanted to take a dog off my hands. For about five minutes it had worked like an open sesame, with everybody in the bar shouting about dogs, and me in the middle of it, but when they found out the truth I had to pretend it was a joke.

'Nay, it's in t' dogs' home!' I called back in the hearty voice. They laughed indulgently.

Freddy Platt winked elaborately at his mates. 'When's ta bahn off to London, Billy?' he called. He started nudging the man next to him and urging: 'Go on, Sam, ask him when he's off to London.'

They were always bringing that one up, too. I had told them months ago, prematurely as it turned out, that I had a job in London waiting for me. I had been gratified, and then alarmed, at the way the story had spread through the pub, like a dangerous fire. They were still at it with the embers.

'When's to bahn off to London, Billy?'

'I'll be going, don't you worry!' They laughed again, shaking their heads. 'He's a case, i'n't he?' said Freddy Platt. 'He is. He's a case.' I gave them the deprecating smile, cornered again into the position of village idiot or licensed clown or whatever it was they imagined me to be. Freddy shouted across the room: 'Has ta fetched that stuff down, Walter?' and they were back with their repertoire of secrets.

I walked through into the concert-room, a hideous cork-floored drill hall with buff walls and fancy strip-lighting fitments that looked like rejects from a luxury liner. The concert was already warming up, with the Clavioline thumping away and an Irish labourer, grasping the microphone as though it were a pint pot, singing, *'Blais this house nya Lard we pray.'* Johnny the waiter moved round the room with his tin tray held high above his head, and the fat women sat at the bow-legged tables eating packets of nuts and knocking back the shorts. Their husbands stood at the long bar at the end of the room, where you didn't have to watch the concert if you didn't want to.

The long bar was where the members of the Ancient Order of Stags or whatever it was gathered on Saturday nights, waiting for their lodge meeting to begin upstairs. They were there now, all lean-faced men calling each other brother, forever shaking hands and digging in their pockets for penny fines. In their own way they were as bad as Freddy Platt and *his* crowd and I gave them the same limp wave and looked away.

There was a patter of applause for the Irish singer, and Johnny the waiter cried: 'Can I 'ave your orders please before the next *turn*!' He started hustling round the room with his tray under his arm and a fistful of silver. Behind me a ponderous voice said: 'Now then, young man!'

I turned round to see another group of Stags padding in from the saloon bar, all holding pints of beer. In the middle of them was Councillor Duxbury, wearing the chain of past grand warden or something. He did not often come to this lodge, and when he did I managed as a rule to avoid him. I was not sure what my status with him was after our encounter on Stradhoughton Moor; I played for safety with a non-committal smile.

One of the men he was with said with heavy jocularity: 'Well, is the worthy brother bahn to give us a turn toneet?'

Councillor Duxbury gave me a solemn wink and said: 'Nay, he is but an untutored apprentice, brother deacon.'

Brother deacon winked too. Practically every man in the pub made a practice of winking before he opened his mouth. 'And what about thee, brother warden? Art thou tutored?'

'Aye, it's not me that wants tutoring.' Councillor Duxbury was looking at me pointedly, and I knew that I was supposed to get some kind of hidden message out of what he was saying. I was wondering already what I had found so understanding about him on Stradhoughton Moor. Then it occurred to me that he had probably heard about Shadrack's audit of the postage book since then.

'Tha'rt initiated, then?' said brother deacon, staggering on with the joke. 'Give t' password.'

'At my initiation I was taught to be cautious. I will letter or half it wi' thee, which you please,' recited Councillor Duxbury.

The Stags spent half their time fooling about in this way, and some of them I knew had long ago stopped speaking in any other manner. Councillor Duxbury and brother deacon were settling down for a long, pedantic cross-talk; but before they had the chance to go rumbling through their passwords, the third man in the group spoke huffily: 'The lodge is not yet tiled, brothers!'

Through the crackling microphone, Johnny the waiter announced: 'Quiet, please! *Can* I 'ave a bit of quiet? And now, two very clever young men who've come all the way over from Dewsbury to entertain us tonight, Bob and *Ha*rry! Quiet now, please!' The two young men with fresh, eager-to-please faces bounded on to the low platform and started miming facetiously to a record of 'Baby it's cold outside'. They were making an elaborate strong-man-and-coy-girl act of it, fluttering with the eyelids and slapping each other, and I found it embarrassing to look at them.

'Well we'll go up and get t' lodge tiled, then, if tha'rt so particular,' said Councillor Duxbury.

'Shall we tak' t' untutored apprentice up wi' us?' said brother deacon, clawing at me playfully. 'Come on, lad, ther'll be someone tha knows up theer.'

'The craft will keep its omnipotent eye on t' untutored apprentice,' said Councillor Duxbury.

They were all winking at each other like maniacs, and shoving each other's elbows. Filled with an accumulation of nausea I muttered: 'Excuse me,' and sidled out of their way. I meant to take refuge in the saloon bar but, hardly knowing what I was doing, I found myself slipping through the first door I could find, and I was back in the public bar. The old voice cried: 'Here he is again – *the boy*!' I stopped, feeling trapped in the haze of faces. I looked wildly around the bar, searching for a beer barrel or something that I could focus my eyes on without any harm coming from it. I saw an old man like a tramp, hobbling about the room trying to sell an armful of comic papers. I gazed at him steadily as though trying to place his blank face.

Out of one of the close, anonymous groups I heard the honking voice of Freddy Platt: 'Ther's thi paper here, Billy! Give 'im t' paper, Sam!'

'Billy's Weekly Liar!' roared somebody else. 'Go on, Sam, give 'im it!'

'He doesn't want it – he's t' editor!'

We had been through this one before, many a time. *Billy's Weekly Liar* was the comic paper that was peddled about the pub on Saturday nights, along with the *War Cry* and the *Empire News*. They would buy one copy between four of them and sit around pointing at the jokes with their stubby fingers. When they saw me coming they would bring out their own old joke.

'*Billy's Weekly Liar*! Here y'are, Billy!' Somebody was trying to shove the paper into my hand.

'Billy Liar!' laughed Freddy Platt. He was shouting at the top of his voice to compete with the noise from the concert-room next door; the miming act was climbing up to a screaming, oscillating crescendo, and it needed nothing but a couple of policemen running about blowing whistles to complete the sudden, hysterical chaos. 'Billy Liar! We'll call 'im that, eh? We'll call 'im that, Sam! Billy Liar. By! Where's thi dog, Billy?'

He did not get any response from me. I could not even see him. I stared sightlessly around the public bar, darting from one object to another without recognising anything. 'He's a case!' shouted Freddy Platt. 'He is, he makes me laugh! By!'

I felt someone prodding me from behind. I staggered a little under the impetus and wondered whether there would be any future in letting myself go on falling until I was flat on my face on the floor and they would have to carry me out into the cool, quiet air. It was Johnny the waiter with his tray loaded with empty glasses and bottle tops. 'You're on next, Billy boy.' Without caring much what I was doing I stumbled back into the concert-room. 'Billy Liar and his talking dog!' shouted Freddy Platt. I whipped round angrily, and saw that the whole lot of them had got up and were following me into the concert-room. I shambled across the cork floor through the troops of women, buckling at the knees in case I should retrieve the idea of dropping in a dead faint.

'All right, now the best of order now! If you please! Next on the bill to entertain us tonight we 'ave a young man who needs no introduction from me. Quiet, please, for our very own Billee *Fish*ah! Break it up small, you lads!'

I climbed up on the platform, with the Clavioline running meaninglessly through the first few bars of 'I want to be happy'. I looked out across the concert-room at all the people, trying to remember the first line of my act but knowing perfectly well that whatever it was, it was nothing to do with them, and whatever they were, it was nothing to do with me. Some of the women at the round, rocking tables stared at me like cows waiting to be milked, but most of them took no notice at all. Freddy Platt and his friends stood at the end of the room by the public bar door, in a swaying, solid group, still swopping their secrets. I was surprised and depressed to see that Bob and Harry, the two young men involved in the miming act, had sat down with a crowd old enough to be their fathers; they were smoking the same Woodbines and drinking the same mild beer. All the people in the concert-room sat so comfortably, as though they had reached a reasonable agreement with life and death, as though they knew all about it, all that there was to know about it.

I put on my funny face and started on the club turn, wishing that I could whistle 'In a Monastery Garden' through my teeth instead, and please everybody.

'Ah'm coortin'.'

A few titters from some of the more impressionable women but, on the whole, dead silence.

'Ah am. Ah'm coortin'.'

I jerked my head round with the well-staged, well-practised pop-eyed, indignant look, as though expecting scorn or laughter or disbelief or some reaction of some kind or another from the audience.

'It's a Wakefield lass.'

I saw the same people, the women, Freddy Platt and Co., and the few customers at the long bar. Most of the Stags had gone upstairs, knocking three times on the door to get themselves let into the lodge; but there was one man standing by himself at the bar counter, dragging on a cigarette and holding his beer as though it had dealt him an injury. I caught his eye and fear, real fear and not a substitute, clutched me. I forgot the act and bent down urgently to where Johnny the waiter was ladling out gin and pep at the table nearest the platform.

'Johnny! Johnny! *What the bloody hell is our old man doing here?*'

Johnny looked up, surprised. 'He's joining t' Stags, it's initiation night,' he whispered. 'Get on wi' t' turn!'

I muttered, 'Jesus Christ Almighty' and straightened up and faced the microphone, feeling as though somebody had just kicked me in the stomach. I had never seen the old man in a pub before, and had come to depend upon him never using the New House. He was looking at me sardonically; so, if it came to that, was the rest of the audience by now. Some of the women were getting restless. I gave the old man a stiff, formal bow and he turned away with a gesture of contempt and embarrassment. Freddy Platt shouted: 'When's ta bringing t' dog on, Billy?' I ran quickly through my lines. Ah'm coortin.' It's a Wakefield lass.

'She does, she comes from Wakefield. She's a nice lass, only she's got one big fault. She stutters.'

There was some untidy sniggering from various parts of the concert-room. In so far as the act would come to life at all, it was beginning to warm up.

'She does, she stutters.'

I gave them the pop-eyed look again, avoiding the old man's eye. I had just blasted him with the Ambrosian repeater gun; so far as I was concerned he was no longer there.

'But she's a very warm-hearted lass, very warm-hearted. She'll do owt for you. And she likes a cuddle. Oh, yes, she likes a cuddle. Only she stutters.

'We were sitting in t' parlour one night, y'know, just t' two of us, and she were sitting there, and I were sitting here, and she looked at me, she looked at me and she says, would you like a nice cuh cuh cuh cuh cuh cuh cuh cuh —— '

The sniggering was well set in by now. The fattest woman of all screamed aloud and the others laughed, this time at her. Freddy Platt was making some kind of noise of his own at the back of the room.

'Would you like a cuh cuh cuh cuh cuh cuh —— '

I suddenly realised, with the old sinking feeling what the low thudding noise I had been hearing for the last minute was. Councillor Duxbury had descended the stairs from the lodge and was clomping deliberately across the concert-room floor towards the gents, the seal of past grand warden swinging round his neck like a prize medal on an old shire horse. He passed within a yard of the old man, but they did not speak to each other.

'Would you like a cuh cuh cuh cuh cup of tea?'

The women shrieked. 'T' record's stuck!' shouted Freddy Platt. I saw Councillor Duxbury off to the door of the lavatory.

'Then she gets all coy and says yes, ah knows thee, ah bet you thought I were going to ask you if you wanted a cuh cuh cuh cuh cuh cup of cocoa!'

I got to the end of the stuttering joke, whatever it was. Councillor Duxbury emerged from the gents, buttoning his flies. He walked slowly over to the old man and stood indecisively at the side of him, as though he had forgotten what it was all about.

'But o' course, ah'm a poor man. Ah can't support her. Ah can't support her. Ah only had one clog on me foot when ah came to Stradhoughton. Only one clog on me foot. But very soon ah were riding about in taxis.'

The two of them, the old man and Councillor Duxbury, stood talking for a moment. The old man glanced in my direction once, but not malevolently. He finished his beer and the two of them set off towards the stairs, the old man hanging back to keep pace with Duxbury. I had no idea why he should be joining the Stags, but it was obvious that as one Stag to another Councillor Duxbury would tell him all that there was to be told about me.

'Ah had to take a taxi because ah only had one clog.'

I was back with the fat women and Freddy Platt and his crowd. I brought out the jokes as I remembered them, trying to bring the act to a finish. Some of the women screeched from time to time, but nobody really cared whether I was on or off the platform. They were beginning to turn round to each other and whisper and light cigarettes, and to pour out beer and hold it studiously to the light, as though I wasn't there at all.

'Any road, this *feller stuttered as well. So he goes up to this bookie and y'know, it were t' right busy time, just before t' last race, and he says, ah've backed ah've backed ah've backed ah've backed ah've backed ah've backed —— '*

'Ah've backed a loser!' shouted Freddy Platt.

'Ah've backed ah've backed ah've backed ah've backed. So t' bookie says, gerron wi' it, ah've not got all day —— '

('Neither 'ave we!')

'So he says ah've backed ah've backed ah've backed ah've backed, So t' bookie says, come on, nark it —— '

'*Nark* it?' exploded Freddy Platt triumphantly. '*Nark* it? That's not Yorkshire!'

'So he says nark it —— '

'That's not Yorkshire! That's London talk! He thinks he's in London!'

'So he says —— '

Freddy Platt's mate, giving an excruciating imitation of a cockney, went: 'Eeyah! Ply the gyme, myte! Caw bloimey!'

The whole thing was getting out of hand. The concert-room was buzzing with talk and laughter, as though they had all just come out of a meeting. They were beginning to nudge each other, nodding in my direction and laughing to themselves. Johnny the waiter was making winding motions with his hand, telling me to get off the platform.

I called back in the bluff, appeasing voice: 'It's all right, ah'm just practising for when ah get to London! Any road, let me finish t' story! *So this bookie says give ower, 'ere's five quid, you can tell me what you've backed after t' race. So t' bloke – this feller – says nay, ah've backed ah've backed ah've backed –* '

There was a gale of laughter, the kind of laugh you get for sheer audacity. Freddy Platt and his friends were beginning to chant: 'Ah've backed ah've backed ah've backed.' Chairs were scraping and people were knocking glasses over and rooting in their handbags, Other people, total strangers, started chanting: 'Ah've backed ah've backed ah've backed.' There was a mood of pandemonium. I was expecting them any minute to start flicking pellets at each other.

'Ah've backed my lorry through thy window,' I finished, almost in a whisper. I jumped down from the platform, spraying the lot of them with the Ambrosian repeater gun. There was a trickle of applause from about four people, but most of them did not even realise I had finished. The pianist did not bother to give me a few bars on the Clavioline, whether of 'I want to be happy' or any other tune. Staggering across the room I tried to remember how many times I had done this club turn in the past; knowing that each occasion would, in retrospect, become a rich, separate source of acute embarrassment. Some of the women looked at me with a kind of compassionate detachment as I passed. They had stared at me in this way before but I had never realised that it was because they knew things I didn't know, because they were involved in basic matters that I had never even heard about.

I made for the nearest door I could see. 'By! *Tha* dropped a clanger there, Billy!' said Freddy Platt. '"Nark it?" Tha didn't learn *that* in Yorkshire! Tha what? By!'

I raised my fist in what he was to imagine was a playful gesture. Up on the platform Johnny the waiter, trying to mend the broken illusions and turn the place back into a concert-room, announced that somebody or other would sing a laughing song. A middle-aged, cocky-looking man in a cloth cap, a seasoned club turn with a full diary of engagements, took the microphone. He began singing in a broad, confident voice.

'Now I think that life is merry,
I think that life is fun,
A short life and a happy one
Is my rule number one,
I laugh when it is raining,
I laugh when it is fine,
You may think I am foolish,
But laughter is my line,
Oh, ha ha ha ha ha ha,
Ha ha ha ha hee,
Ha ha ha ha ha ha,
Ho ho ho ho hee.'

'When's ta bahn off to London, Billy?' cried Freddy Platt. Some of the women nearest to him turned round and went 'Sssh!' They were all watching the singer, their potato crisps untouched. The place was already transformed.

'Billy Liar and his talking dog, the well-known double act!'

'Sssh!'

'Ha ha ha ha ha ha,
Ho ho ho ho hee,
Oh, ha ha ha ha ha ha,
Ha ha ha ha hee.'

I blundered out of the pub and into the car park. I did not stop running until I was clear of Clogiron Lane.

Chapter Ten

The Roxy was the last splash of light before Stradhoughton petered out and the moors took over. It was supposed to be a suburban amenity or something; at any rate its red, humming neon sign spluttered out the words 'Come Dancing' six nights a week, and all the grown-up daughters of the cold new houses round about converged on it in their satin frocks, carrying their dance shoes in paper bags advertising pork pies. Youths who had come from all over Stradhoughton for the catch sat around on the low brick banisters by the entrance, combing their hair and jeering at each other.

I approached the place warily, along the shadows, in case Rita was among the girls who promenaded up and down the cracked concrete forecourt, waiting for their escorts to come and pay for them in. I was still full of the evening's fiasco, with selected incidents from it swimming in and out of my head like shoals of bright fish, but as I stepped into the pool of light outside the Roxy I felt an overwhelming relief that another experience was finished with and not still to come. A girl I had once known was waiting by the entrance; I said, 'Hiya, Mavis!' boldly as I passed. I had once written her a poem comparing her bosom with twin melons, and it was always fairly embarrassing to meet her nowadays. But it was something fresh to think about anyway. She said, 'Lo, Billy,' and I walked almost cheerfully up to the paybox.

Inside the Roxy it was hot and bright and, as Stamp had once put it, smelling like a ladies' bog. The foyer, separated from the dance floor by a certain amount of cream fretwork and a lot of big plants, was crowded with the same kind of youths I had seen in the X-L Disc Bar earlier; they were all pulling at their tight clean collars and working their heads round like tortoises. Their girl friends queued for the lavatory, and emerged with their zip-boots and their headscarves discarded, each one making a sort of furtive entry like a butterfly that has turned into a caterpillar. I surveyed this scene with the usual distaste, hunching my shoulders and adopting the attitude of the visiting poet; I was not inclined at this moment towards the bit of No. 1 thinking, fairly standard in this quarter, where I took the floor to a cha-cha with one of the professional exhibition dancers who looked so much like wardresses. I could not see Liz anywhere. I wandered through the fretwork Moorish archway on to the fringe of the dance floor.

The floor was already crowded, with the revolving ball of mirrors overhead catching a hideous violet spotlight and dancing the colours over the pimpled face of, to name the first person I saw, Stamp. He was doing a smirking foxtrot with some girl in a tight, red wool dress; when he turned her in my direction for a piece of cross-stepping that nearly had the pair of them flat on their backs, I saw that his partner was Rita. From her slightly dazed expression, open-mouthed and cloudy-eyed – a kind of facial rigor mortis that touched her whenever she got inside a dance hall – I guessed that Rita had been here about half an hour. I was a little pained that she had not bothered to wait outside for me – she was, after all, still my fiancée, or thought she was – but I was glad to see that Stamp was taking care of her. He looked a little drunk; but that was his problem and not mine. They glided past without seeing me.

At the bandstand Arthur's friends, the Rockets, blew their muted instruments behind little plywood pulpits, the drummer brushing away and grinning round at everybody as though he knew them. Arthur himself, wearing a blue American-cut suit, was swaying about in front of the stick-shaped microphone, waiting to sing. He looked like Danny Kaye or somebody doing a relaxed season at the Palladium, and I could not help admiring his poise and the professional way he stood there doing nothing. I was glad that he had not seen my performance at the New House. I caught his eye and waved to him, a half-wave arrested before it began. Arthur gave me the same mock bow that, in his situation, I had given to the old man; but he did it with a casual dash that made it part of the act.

The people on the dance floor hung around holding hands limply as one tune finished and the Rockets started on the next. Arthur, splaying his hands out, began to sing. '*Yooo're my – ev'rthing, ev'ry li'l thing I know-oo.'* He always affected an American accent when he sang. I disliked it, but I had to admit it was good. Then swaying couples brushed past me and, as Stamp and Rita came round for the second time, I began to pick my way upstairs to the balcony.

Liz was sitting by herself at one of the wickerwork tables, gazing down over the dance floor with her chin resting on her plump arms, and smiling happily to herself. I sat down without saying anything to her. She reached out her hand across the table and I took it.

'Late,' said Liz reprovingly as the song finished.

'Yes,' I said. 'I've had an exciting day.'

'I bet you have. Where've you been?'

'Oh, here and there —— '

'– up and down,' said Liz, joining in the chant.

'– round and about.' This was a common exchange between us. We used it most when I brushed, without actually asking, on the subject of where Liz kept disappearing to for weeks at a time. I took her hand again. She was still wearing her old black skirt, but with a fresh white blouse. Her green suède jacket hung on the back of the basket chair. I was happy to be with her; it was like being in a refuge, her beaming, comfortable presence protecting me from the others.

'Tell me some plans,' said Liz luxuriously.

'What plans?'

'Any plans. *Your* plans. You *al*ways have plans. What are you going to do next?'

'I'm thinking of going to London,' I said.

'Only thinking?'

'Well, *go*ing. Soon, anyway.'

'When's soon?' Liz and I could talk like this for hours, batting the same moonbeams backwards and forwards across the table, enjoying ourselves enormously.

'Well, *soon*.'

'That sounds remote. Why not now?'

'Difficult,' I said.

'No, it's easy. You just get on a train and four hours later, there you are in London.'

'Easy for you,' I said. 'You've had the practice. Liz ——?' We were both leaning over the balcony, our hands dovetailed together. On the packed dance floor, near the bandstand, there was a small arena of space where Stamp and Rita, gyrating dangerously, were working out a dance of their own invention. They were both looking down at the floor to see what their feet were doing.

'Yes?' said Liz.

'Stamp calls you Woodbine Lizzie,' I said.

'You should hear what I call Stamp,' said Liz.

I scanned the dance floor idly, and then sat up with a jolt. I had once read about Shepheard's Hotel in Cairo that if you sat there long enough everyone you knew would pass your table. The Roxy was this sort of establishment too and why someone didn't blow *that* up I could never understand, because the next person I picked out, bouncing along the pine-sprung floor with fresh chalk on his uppers was Shadrack himself, doing the quickstep as it might be performed by a kangaroo. The girl he was with, just to complete the wild pattern of coincidence, was Mavis, the one with the twin-melon bosom I had spoken to outside the Roxy. They were no doubt talking about me. Stamp and Rita were still milling around near the bandstand, and I suddenly knew for certain that somewhere on the premises the Witch, too, was waiting, breathing through her nose and swinging her skirt and looking in general as though she had come to dance the Gay Gordons over a couple of swords.

'Let's go for a walk,' I said.

'Soon,' said Liz, mocking me.

Downstairs the drums rolled and Arthur came to the microphone, lifting his hands to quell the faint suggestion of applause. He put his face close to the mike and, in his half-American accent, began the smooth talk that went down so well.

'Lazengenelmen, are we all happy? Thank you, madam. Next week at the Roxy we have another all-pop night, feat'ring the Rockets, that golden songstress Jeannie Lewis – Jeannie Lewis, I'm not saying she's fat but she's the only girl I know who when she has a chest complaint, she gets her treatment wholesale – and by popular request, yours truly. Success! *Lazengenelmen, when I came to Stradhoughton I only had one clog. Now I ride around in taxis. I have to take a taxi, I've only got one clog.'*

There were waves of relaxed laughter for Arthur, a cabaret sort of atmosphere that suited him perfectly. Jeannie Lewis, the singer, was sitting on a cane chair by the band, heaving her sequined bosom. Arthur waited for silence, clicking his fingers and smiling confidently.

'And now a special treat for us all. I want to continue the dance with a little number which I wrote in conjunction with my very good friend Billy Fisher. Where are you, Billy?' The spotlight played hopefully about the floor, while the Rockets' drummer made a facetious clacking on the kettle-drum.

'That's *you*!' said Liz excitedly.

'I'm all right,' I muttered, hiding my face.

'Well I know he's out there somewhere,' said Arthur. *'Maybe he's celebrating the big news, because I know you'll all be glad to know that Billy has just landed himself a big job in London, writing scripts for that verywellknown comedian Danny Boon! I'm sure we wish him all the best in the world.'*

'You stupid *cow*!' I hissed. There was a bit of desultory applause, and one or two of the people on the balcony who knew me slightly looked at me curiously. In spite of it all, I tried to look reasonably famous.

'Now on with the dance with the little number by Billy Fisher and yours truly – "Can't get along without you"!' He said it in the coy way that television disc jockeys have, putting the eye on a random girl when he pronounced this soft word 'you'.

'I wish he'd stop calling himself yours truly,' I said through my teeth.

'Shush,' said Liz. 'I want to hear your song.'

The band struck up far too slowly for the number and Arthur, the wry creases in his forehead, began to sign.

> *'Soon you will be saying good-bye,*
> *Just let me mention that I*
> *Can't get along without you.*
> *You seem to have changed with the moon,*
> *Now my heart beats out of tune,*
> *Can't get along without you.'*

I squinted craftily at Liz, hoping she would think the song was dedicated to her. Then I looked down over the balcony at the people dancing below. Nobody seemed to be taking much notice of the song, and in fact Arthur's American accent had become so pronounced that it was difficult to understand what he was singing about. Shadrack and the girl Mavis had vanished, and so had Rita. Stamp was loitering on the brass-rimmed edge of the dance floor, obviously trying to find some way of sabotaging the number. I thought Arthur was doing that effectively himself.

'I want to discover
If I'm to blame,
Because as a lover
You're not the same so tell me why.'

'He's singing it all wrong,' I muttered, getting up. 'Anyway, I suppose I'd better go and congratulate him.' Liz wrinkled her nose at me, and I ran self-consciously down the stairs, keeping my eyes peeled for people who might want to see me.

'Please tell me why we must part,
Darling it's breaking my heart,
Can't get along without you.'

I reached the bandstand as Arthur, his arms outstretched, touched the last note. The Rockets went straight into 'American Patrol' and he jumped down, flexing his shoulders and waving to his friends.

'And then I wrote —— ' I began, striking a dramatic pose for the beginning of our song-writer routine.

'Ah yes, and do you remember the little tune that went something like this,' said Arthur, clutching his heart with one hand and cupping the other to his ear.

'You made me love you, I didn't want to do it, I didn't want to do it,' I sang dutifully in the cracked phonograph voice.

'To think I wrote that song on the back of a menu in a fish restaurant —— '

'– and today that menu is worth hundreds of pounds.'

'Yes, the price of fish rose steeply between the two wars,' said Arthur, finishing the routine. But it was not the usual thing between me and him; this time he was talking loudly, addressing an audience, the admiring girls who stood around the band giggling and doing little solo jigs.

'And then I wrote —— ' he said, looking round. I drew him on one side.

'Bloody good, man,' I said. 'How did you manage to persuade them to let you sing it?'

'In your honour,' said Arthur, and now that we had dropped the routine I thought that he was talking in a curiously formal sort of voice.

'Bloody good. Wish you hadn't announced that bit about Danny Boon, though.'

'Why not. It's all fixed up, isn't it?' For the first time, I noticed the slight glint of malice in his eye and the corner of his lower lip twitching.

'Yes, course it is. Only I just didn't want anyone to know just yet, that's all. We ought to get that song recorded and send it up to a publisher.'

'We're going to do it,' said Arthur, meaning him and the Rockets, and also meaning without any help from me.

'Only one thing,' I said in the light voice. 'You want to sing it with a bit less of an American accent.'

Arthur turned to me full-face, and I got the whole effect of the studied, indifferent approach.

'I'll sing it with a *Yorkshire* accent if you like.'

I flared up. 'I don't want you to sing it with *any* flaming accent. Just sing it as it's flaming well written, that's all.'

'Listen, boy, if I sang that song the way you wrote it it'd clear the bleeding hall. You've still got a lot to learn, cocker.'

'Oh, for Christ's sake —— '

Arthur nodded his chin. 'Yes, I can see them taking *you* down a peg or two when you get to London. *If* you get to London, I should say. Anyway, don't tell *me* how to sing, matey. Anyone'd think you were going to work for bleeding Glenn Miller.'

'Oh, it's like that, is it?' I said.

'Yes, it's like that. And another thing. I don't know what bloody lies you've been telling my mother about the Witch being this bloody sister of yours, but she's been doing her nut all afternoon. So bloody lay off, for Christ sake.'

He strode back to the bandstand, grabbing the microphone and switching on the American voice. *'And now folks*, by *request – the Hokey-Cokey!'* I turned away, miserable and depressed.

I had almost reached the stairs to the balcony when I saw Stamp leering over the banisters, beckoning his grimy fingers at me. I swung back abruptly and made for the cafeteria under the balcony, at the side of the dance floor. I meant to lose myself for a few minutes among the squealing girls scoffing cream buns and spilling lemonade down their dresses. I hurried through the rows of enamelled tables towards the dark corner by the band's changing-room, and it was only when I was in the middle of it that I realised what kind of bear-pit I had walked into down here. Immediately in front of me stood the Witch in a revolting green blouse and tartan skirt. She was confronting Rita, and Rita's vivid red dress seemed to have been designed especially to set off the miniature silver cross on its silver chain round her neck, and the engagement ring that she brandished on her finger.

'That's *my* cross,' I heard the Witch say in her loud, clear voice.

My heart, familiar with its duty on occasions such as this, did a full cartwheel. I dodged behind a sort of Corinthian column that was holding the balcony up, but too late to avoid the cold eye of the Witch.

'Talk of the devil,' she said coolly.

Rita turned round. 'Oo, look what's jumped out of the corned beef,' she said in her grating voice. She looked flushed and bewildered.

I said faintly: 'What's this – a deputation?' I skimmed through my mind, more or less in despair, to see if I could find a piece of skilful double-talk, aimed at their different intellectual levels, that would succeed in fooling them both. I opened my mouth to speak but I felt the yawn welling up in my throat and I finished up standing there with my mouth open, gaping at them. 'What's up with him, is he catching flies or summat?' said Rita. It was obviously too late for the academic niceties, anyway.

'May I ask why you gave my cross to this – girl?' asked the Witch without any preamble.

My first thought was: 'May I ask why you said you'd given it back to your cousin?' But I still hankered after the subtle approach. 'Yes, it *is* very similar, isn't it?' I said.

'It's my cross. It's got the tooth-mark on it where you bit it that day when you made that ridiculous scene.'

'Do you mean that day at Ilkley, which I am sure Rita is anxious to hear about?' I said, with the intention of embarrassing her.

'It's my cross,' said the Witch.

'No it isn't,' I said. 'You gave yours back to your cousin. I just happen to have one similar. If you want to know, your cousin got it from me in the first place.'

'Oh. So you make a *prac*tice of giving these things away, do you?'

'No. I don't make a *prac*tice of it. I just happened to have half a dozen of them to spare. They're what Unitarians wear when they're dead,' I said. It was only a matter of time before the Witch realised who was wearing her engagement ring, and I was beginning to gabble a bit.

'And another thing,' the Witch said. 'Which one of us is supposed to be coming to tea at your house tomorrow?'

'Well neither of you, I'm afraid,' I said, giving them each the frank smile. 'We did hope to have a sort of family party – there were a lot of people coming, including yourselves – only the old man's been called away to Harrogate and he won't be back until Monday.'

'I suppose he's gone to a naval reunion,' said the Witch with her heavy sarcasm. She turned to Rita. 'You know his father's supposed to be a retired sea captain, don't you?'

'Thought he was supposed to be a cobbler or summat,' said Rita.

They started chewing the fat about what the old man did for a living. The Witch, in her bottle-green blouse, stood there looking like the cub-mistress Stamp claimed to have ravished on passion pills. A happy thought struck me, the first happy thought of the evening. I felt in my pocket for the little black beads that were still spilled there. I scooped up a handful, about a dozen or fourteen of them. On the table nearest to us, next to the Witch's handbag and the pile of blood oranges that she had got in as a treat for herself, there was a cup of black coffee, untouched. I moved my hand behind me and, as the two of them got on to the subject of the imaginary budgerigar, I unloaded the fistful of passion pills into the Witch's coffee.

'And now, if it's not too much to ask,' said the Witch, 'perhaps you'll tell us which one of us you invited to the Roxy tonight.'

'Oh, my God,' I said. 'Why don't you ask Rita why she's wearing your engagement ring?' I strode rapidly away, leaving them both open-mouthed as though being filmed at the end of a comedy sequence. I charged through the cafeteria to the foot of the balcony stairs. Stamp, still clinging hold of the banisters, clawed at me as I passed. He was definitely drunk.

'Go to hell, Stamp,' I said curtly.

'*You've* had it,' he said thickly, grabbing my sleeve. '*You've* had it.'

'Keep your mucky hands to yourself.'

'You've *had* it,' drooled Stamp. 'Just been talking to Shadrack. You've *had* it, Fisher.'

I pulled his hand angrily off my sleeve. 'Well you get your hands off my cowing, mucking, stinking *sleeve*!'

'You've had it,' he mumbled, sinking down on the stairs. I ran up two at a time and found Liz still sitting contentedly, looking over the balcony.

'Sorry I was so long. Let's go for a walk.'

She looked up and smiled. 'You're looking het up.'

'I'm feeling het up,' I said. I edged over to where she was sitting to check that she could not have seen what had been going on. 'I've just had an almighty barney with Arthur about the song. He finished up threatening to sing it with a Yorkshire accent.'

'Well, he could do worse,' said Liz judiciously.

I sat down, breathing deeply, glad of any opportunity for a bit of normal conversation. The band was playing a soft waltz and there was something soothing about the bobbing heads below us.

'Don't say you're another of these Yorkshire fanatics,' I said.

'No. But there's lots of nice things in Yorkshire. Nice people. To name only one,' she said, squeezing my hand.

'Which is why you keep leaving it, I suppose?'

'Could be.'

To break the silence I said: 'I was talking to that bloke who does the Man o' the Dales' column in the *Echo* the other day —— '

'Who? Do you mean John Hardcastle?' Liz broke in. 'I *know* him.' She knew everybody.

'That's him,' I said with the sinking feeling. 'At least, I *think* it was him. *One* of the blokes on the *Echo*, anyway. We were going over all this satanic mills lark that he's always doing, and *I* said, Dark Satanic mills I can put up with, they're part of the picture. But when it comes to dark satanic power stations, dark satanic housing estates and dark satanic dance halls —— '

'That's good. You ought to use that.'

'So *he* said, "That's the trouble with the youngsters, you want —— "'

'Youngsters? *He's* got a nerve! He's not much older than you are! Are you sure it was John Hardcastle?'

'Oh, for God's sake,' I said desperately. 'A big chap with a moustache – is that him?'

'That's right,' said Liz calmly. 'He's sitting over there.' She nodded casually to a young man with a crowd of people three or four tables away, handlebar moustache and all. Why wasn't Man o' the Dales an old man? And why the handlebar moustache? He looked up, saw Liz and waved. I sat back, exhausted. By now I would not have been surprised to see Councillor Duxbury himself, dancing the Boston Two-Step down below and change out of fourpence.

'Let's go for a walk,' I said weakly.

'Don't you want to have a chat with John?'

Over the tannoy, breaking into the music, a crackling voice announced: *'Mist' William Fisher. Mist' William Fisher. Wanted on the telephone. Mist' William Fisher. Than' you.'*

'Mr William Fisher, wanted on the telephone,' said Liz.

My palms gritty with sweat, I gripped the balcony rail and peered into the bright depths of the dance floor. As in some maniac kaleidoscope I could see Arthur, looking belligerent, about to sing; the Witch striding purposefully out of the cafeteria with her handbag swinging on her shoulder; Rita, standing around looking dazed; to the left, Stamp, standing at the bottom of the staircase, and Shadrack brushing past him. I saw them, or thought I saw them, all in the same shrieking moment, and looking up, there was the youthful Man o' the Dales, glaring with what looked like suspicion at our table. I had a sudden histrionic urge to stand up on my chair and shout: 'Ladies and gentlemen, here are my fountain pen and my suède shoes. Crucify me the modern way!'

'Mist' William Fisher, wanted on the telephone.'

'Let's go for a walk,' I said. I felt a hand on the back of my chair. I looked up, and I was not surprised to see Shadrack bending over us, flashing his yellow teeth and breathing his bad breath.

'*Could* I have a word with you, Fisher?'

I stood up, feeling punchdrunk. 'Next for shaving,' I said hysterically.

Shadrack turned solicitously to Liz. 'You *will* excuse us for a moment?' She smiled at him. He took me over to the top of the stairs, holding my arm in an alarmingly friendly way.

'Look, this is neither the time *nor* the place, of *course*,' he began confidentially. 'But I just thought I'd better have a word with you about our conversation this afternoon.'

'Oh, yes?' I said, swallowing.

'Yes. The fact is, under the circ'stances we think it prob'ly a good idea if you didn't come in on Monday after all. Prob'ly if you didn't come in until we sent for you. I just thought I'd let you know.'

'Oh. Does that mean —— ?'

'No, I'm vair much afraid it doesn't mean you've finished with us. Not by a long chalk. I'm afraid you've still got a lot of explaining to do, Fisher.'

'Oh?' I seemed to be beginning every sentence with 'Oh.'

'Yes, I'm afraid it's come to light that you've been carrying on in an alarming fashion for a vair lengthy period of time. An al*arm*ing fashion. To say the least of it. Anyway, the upshot is, we want you to regard yourself as being temp'rarily suspended until we can get it all cleared up.'

He released my arm.

'As I say, this is neither the time nor the place, we realise that. I don't want to stop you enjoying yourself tonight, far from it. But you've got a lot of vair serious explaining to do, sooner or later.'

'"Have a good holiday, Jenkins, I've got some bad news for you when you get back,"' I muttered.

'Wha'? What's that?'

'It was a cartoon,' I said unhappily. 'In the paper.'

'Yes, I'm vair much afraid you think too *much* about cartoons,' said Shadrack. He gave me a strange look and went off down the stairs. I watched the tail of his hacking jacket flapping after him, and murmured *'Bastard'* under my breath.

'Mist' William Fisher, wanted on the telephone.'

I beckoned to Liz, and followed Shadrack at a respectful distance down the stairs.

Chapter Eleven

It was quiet outside the Roxy. The evening was warm, but on the crisp side. The sodium lamps were beginning to flicker on and off dismally. The old gaffers who manned the Alderman Burrows memorial bench at the abandoned tram terminus were beginning to crane themselves stiffly to their feet and adjust their mufflers. The last children had left the piles of builders' sand that marked every exit from Stradhoughton, warning of new territorial ambitions in the way of brittle new roads across the moors.

I stood at the entrance to the Roxy, looking at the showcases full of cracked, shiny photographs and the glue-streaked placards advertising the Autumn Leaf Ball. There was one showcase devoted to the Miss Stradhoughton contest and Rita, with her cardboard crown and her satin sash, smiled toothily down at me. On the broad brick steps, the commissionaire in his threadbare uniform, dry-cleaned to a thin blue and tied with an army webbing belt dyed navy, eyed passing youths with his fixed, policeman's stare. Two of them, shiny-haired and wearing dazzle ties, strolled self-consciously up towards the paybox. I recognised them as friends of Stamp from the crowd he had been with at the X-L Disc Bar that afternoon.

The commissionaire moved forward. 'Not tonight, my friends,' he said, putting his arm out. 'Not after last week.'

'Why, what's up?' said one of the youths.

'Never mind what's up, or what's down. You don't come in, that's Mr Bottomley's strict orders.'

'After you with Mr Bottomley,' said the other youth.

'We're not coming in, we just want to get a mate out,' said the first one.

'You're getting nobody out,' said the commissionaire. The two youths retired into the shadows.

I looked up the blue-carpeted foyer at the cluster of girls gossiping outside the Ladies, and saw them part to let Liz through. Some of them stared after her. I noticed, not for the first time, how scruffy she was in her old suède jacket and her dusty black skirt, and it occurred to me that I had rarely, if ever, seen her wearing anything else. She came and went in her green suède coat as though it were a uniform or something, and even when I pictured her at the celebration parade after the November riots in Ambrosia, she was still wearing it.

She came and stood beside me, by the showcases.

'Miss Stradhoughton,' she said mechanically.

'They gave the title to the wrong girl,' I said with a clumsy attempt at gallantry.

We strolled away from the Roxy and the block of tobacconists' shops, chemists and hairdressers that was built in with it, and over the waste ground to the New Road. We walked up New Road past the Houghtondale Arms, the bus sheds and the crematorium and then, where the dump of cracked drainpipes and the crusty little hills of tar marked the last gasp of housing development, we turned into the unadopted road that led down into Foley Bottoms.

At some point during the evening, probably in the flight from the pub concert-room, I had started walking like a man with flat feet, and I was trying hard to stop it. 'Do you find life complicated?' I said as we walked along. I was long past caring one way or the other about anything very much, and what I said was the first thing that came into my head.

'Hmm-hmm,' said Liz happily.

I said: 'I wish it was something you could tear up and start again. Life, I mean. You know, like starting a new page in an exercise book.'

'Well, it's been done,' said Liz. 'Turning over a new leaf.'

'I turn over a new leaf every day,' I said. 'But the blots show through.' I was rather pleased with this.

We came to the end of the unadopted road and crossed over the broken-down chestnut fencing and the backwash of old bricks and bottles that was the entrance to Foley Bottoms.

'Why are you walking like that?' said Liz.

'Like what?'

'Sort of leaning forwards as though you were on roller skates.'

About half a dozen selected falsehoods skimmed through

my mind, ranging from bad shoes to middle ear disease. 'I'm pretending I've got flat feet,' I said at length.

'Fathead.'

Stradhoughton clung tenaciously on to the woods for the first few yards: old prams, cement bags flapping, an electricity sub-station, the trees dying on their feet. But wading through the soggy cardboard boxes and the rust-rimmed bicycle wheels we came to the woods with the acorns falling and the ferns waist-high and green about us.

'I turn over a new leaf every day,' I said. 'But the blots show through the page.'

'Well,' said Liz. 'Perhaps a new leaf isn't good enough. Perhaps you need to turn over a new volume.'

She was even better than I was at carrying metaphor to inscrutable lengths. I thought of pursuing the theme a little further, and was weaving a pleasant fancy about trying not only a new volume but a new library, when Liz started on the problem afresh with an entirely new set of illustrations.

'You know, my lad, the trouble with you is that you're – what's the word – introspective? You're like a child at the edge of a paddling pool. You want very much to go in, but you think so much about whether the water's cold, and whether you'll drown, and what your mother will say if you get your feet wet —— '

I hesitated to go with her into the paddling pool zone, which seemed to me to be fraught with peril, but there was nothing for it but to interrupt her.

'All I'm doing is wondering whether to dive or swim,' I said obscurely.

'Perhaps you need a coach,' said Liz, giving me the sly glance. It was perfectly apparent where this one was leading to, and I decided to leave her floundering in her own paddling pool for the time being. We picked our way over the low blackberry branches in silence.

I searched around in my mind for some fresh nonsense to keep us pleasantly occupied. I felt a quick gust of warmth for Liz for her readiness to go so far with me along the well-trodden paths of fantasy. I decided to try her on the London theme.

'Do you know why I'm so fascinated by London?' I said.

'No, Mr Bones, why are you so fascinated by London?' She was not consciously imitating Arthur.

'A man can lose himself in London.' I said. 'London is a big place. It has big streets and big people —— ' I tailed off, because she would not be drawn, and in any case I had forgotten the end of the sentence. Liz stopped abruptly, and I turned back to face her, expecting the sudden, rash embrace that was a feature of her impetuous temperament.

But she folded her arms and looked at me with her inscrutable, chubby smile that only faintly looked as though, like the Witch before her, she had practised it in a mirror.

'Billy?'

'Uh-huh?'

'Tell me something?'

I said in the soft voice: 'Of course.'

'Do you really know Man o' the Dales?'

In the hard, defiant voice: 'Course I do.'

'Really and truly?'

'Well, know him, it depends what you mean by *know* him. I've *met* him —— '

'Count five and tell the truth,' said Liz. It was an old recipe of hers, and one that I always found distasteful. I said in the high-pitched voice, putting an elaborate hand to my heart, 'I cannot tell a lie, I've never met the man.' The phrase, 'I've never met the man' was just not suited to the range of voice I had chosen, and the whole thing sounded forced and riduculous.

Liz grinned composedly. 'You *are* a fool.'

I wiped the whole matter out with the repeater gun levelled at Man o' the Dales, and we walked on. 'Perhaps I need to turn over a new paddling pool,' I said.

'Write that down,' said Liz, just as Arthur would have said.

Foley Bottoms was largely a botanic clump of nothing, but just before you started getting out of the woods again and on your way to the Strad Lee housing estate – a hideous zoo of orange brick which it would have done Man o' the Dales a power of good to walk through, cobblestones, handlebar moustache and all – there was a knoll or hill of what I always thought of as picnic grass, a kind of lush, tropical green velvet that looked as though you could buy it by the yard in Marks and Spencers. It was a regular custom for me to stop here with whoever it was, Liz, Rita or the Witch; thereafter the custom would vary according to the personality involved. With Rita, it was the film finale clinch prior to sinking down on the grass; with the Witch, a moment of studied casualness in which we both sat down apparently independently, about a yard from one another. I wondered how the Witch was getting on with her cupful of passion pills. In the case of Liz, part of the regular custom was to hold each other at arm's length, scrutinising faces and then, as at a given signal, sit down.

'Who d'you love?' said Liz.

'Thee, lass,' I said, finding refuge in the Duxbury dialect.

'Yes, it sounds like it, doesn't it?'

'Ah do, lass.'

'Say it properly, then.'

'I do, Liz, I do,' I said soberly, and wondering if I meant it. I knelt down on the grass and reached my arm up to her. Liz remained standing.

'What about Barbara?'

So rarely did I think about the Witch under her given name that I had to think for a minute who Barbara was when she was at home.

'Well what about her?'

'Well *what* about her?' said Liz. I began pulling at her hands, trying to decide whether to pass the ball back again with another 'Well what about her?' Finally I said: 'All over.'

'You've said *that* before.'

'I know. This time the goose is cooked.' I did not explain whose goose I had in mind. I tightened my grip on her hands and pulled her down, so successfully that she fell on top of me. This should have been the signal for the beginning of some rural by-play but in fact the weight of her knocked me sprawling and by the time I had recovered she was sitting beside me, lighting a cigarette – a delaying trick as annoying in its way as the Witch's oranges.

'I want to marry you, you know, Billy,' Liz said, holding her cigarette to a blade of grass.

I said: 'I know, Liz, I know. We will, one day.'

'Not one day. Now.'

The idea of actually getting married now was so incomprehensible to me that I thought it was part of some new ritual, and I played along with it.

'Tonight?'

'Next week will do. Before you go to London. Or when you get there. Whichever you prefer.'

I began plucking at the glass buttons of her blouse, imagining the court scene where my mother, weeping, opposed my application to marry. The unfastening of Liz's blouse had become more or less routine affair and it was done in a detached way, rather as if I were helping her off with her coat.

'I think I get engaged a bit too often,' I said.

'I don't want to get engaged. I want to get married.'

'Is that why you keep sloping off every few weeks, because you want to get married?'

'I want to get married,' said Liz stubbornly.

'All right,' I said. 'All right.'

By now I had begun to grow fairly absent-minded in my responses, for it had suddenly struck me that there was somebody in the bushes, listening to us. There was no wind, but every so often one of the rhododendrons behind us would rustle and there would be a crackling of twigs. I looked up sharply, but there was nothing to see.

'How do you mean, all right?' said Liz. 'I've just pro*posed* to you, and you say all right. Aren't you supposed to say this is so sudden, or yes, or something?'

I was groping for some obscure phrase that would comfort her and at the same time leave me uncommitted. I distinctly saw something moving in the bushes behind us. The notion that the Witch had followed us here and was taking everything down in her faultless Gregg shorthand possessed me with an unpleasant vividness.

'If I'm going to dive in,' I said, 'I think it might as well be at the deep end.'

Even if the Witch had got down this remark satisfactorily, there was little that she could make of it in a breach of promise trial. *'Now Mr Fisher, according to these notes you said that if you were going to dive in, it might as well be at the deep end. Now what did you mean by that?'* I got Liz's blouse out of her skirt and began stroking her, like a cat.

Liz screwed her eyes up tightly in the way she did when she was going to say something she thought brazen. Without seeing, she stubbed her cigarette out on the grass.

'You know what you wanted me to do that night on Stradhoughton Moor, and I said another night?'

I remembered very well the cold night on Stradhoughton Moor, in the old folks' shelter, the night before Liz had last disappeared. On that night I had actually proposed, a pretend proposal that we had used for kindling, toasting our hands on it until the early hours when, stiff with cold, we wandered home quietly, the future spent like fireworks.

'I remember,' I said. My heart had begun to beat swiftly. Stamp's phrase, 'Are you getting it regular?' sprang irreverently back into my head. The bushes stirred again, and this time I thought that it might be Stamp himself with his German camera, fitted with infra-red. Either him or the Witch with a portable tape recorder, one or the other.

'Well,' said Liz. 'It's another night tonight, isn't it?'

I kissed her eyes meditatively. So far our relations had been on a thus-far-and-no-further basis, frustrating to both of us but of such a well-established pattern that it came as a slow shock to suggest that the barriers now be taken down.

'Are you sure?' I said, clearing my throat. She nodded, her face full of meaning. Out in the rhododendron bushes the Witch put on another spool. A new notion, that Shadrack was crouching there with a warrant for my arrest, seized me for a moment, then I put it aside to deal with current problems.

'Er – what do you think we ought to do about, you know, babies?'

'Have them,' said Liz luxuriously. 'Lots and lots of them.'

'No, I mean tonight. I mean, I haven't got – you know.'

'It's all right,' said Liz. I peered unhappily out into the bushes. The Witch turned up her volume control, Stamp changed his film and Shadrack crouched forward in the dusk, licking his lips. Liz nestled plumply up to me and bit my ear. We held each other helplessly, doing nothing, the passion seeping away at a dangerous rate.

Liz said: 'Billy?'

'Uh-huh?'

'Ask you something?'

'Uh-huh.'

She screwed up her eyes again and said: 'Do you know what virgo intacta means?'

'Yes.'

'Well. I'm not.'

I sat there quietly, listening. Something had gone wrong with the Witch's tape recorder. Stamp and Shadrack, fiddling with the batteries were adjusting it for her. 'No,' I said finally. 'I somehow didn't think you were.'

'Want me to tell you about it?'

'No.'

I began to fondle her breast, spanning it in my hand and pressing gently with each finger in turn, compulsively. Liz began to breathe heavily and to tremble out of all proportion to the ardour I thought I was drumming up. 'Tell me about it,' I said.

'No, not now.'

'Tell me about it.'

Liz sat up, almost impatiently, pulling her suède coat around her. She stared out into the darkness. Then she began to trace little circles in the grass with her fingers.

'You think that's why I'm always going away, don't you?' she said.

I shrugged, saying and thinking nothing.

'Ask me where I've been for the past five weeks.'

'Does the geographical location make any difference?' I said with simulated bitterness, hoping to keep it all on this same sparring level.

'No, I don't suppose it does,' said Liz. I reached out and touched her breast under her coat, but it was cold and lifeless. She began to speak in a rhythmical, reasoning sort of prose, as though she had rehearsed all the words before she met me.

'Every so often I just want to go away. It's not you, Billy, I want to be here with you. It's the town. It's the people we know. I don't like knowing everybody, or becoming a part of things – do you see what I mean?'

We had been over this before, but from a different route. It had never led so beautifully into the point of contact between us. I began to feel excited, as though on the verge of a discovery.

'What I'd like is to be invisible,' said Liz. 'You know, to do everything without people knowing, and not having to worry about them, not having to ex*plain* all the time. That's why I so enjoyed that night on Stradhoughton Moor. We were both invisible. We —— '

'Liz,' I said urgently. 'Liz, listen, listen.' I took her hands, trembling almost, and began to speak rapidly, leaving staccato, deliberate pauses between my words.

'Liz, do you know what I do? When I want to feel invisible?' I had no experience of wanting to feel invisible, but the text was perfect. I was doctoring my words as I went along, quickly and carefully. 'I've never told anybody. I have a sort of – well, it's an imaginary country, where I go. It has its own people —— '

'Do you do that? I *knew* you would,' cried Liz triumphantly. 'I knew you would. Why are we so alike, Billy? I can read your thoughts. A town like Stradhoughton, only somewhere over by the sea, and we used to spend the whole day on the beach. That's what I used to think about.'

I was full of excitement, frustrated, painful excitement at not being able to tell her properly, yet at the same time knowing she would understand it, knowing that she would *know*. I wanted to drag her into my mind and let her loose in it, free to pick and choose.

I began counting to myself to slow myself down, and said, only half-feverishly:

'This is more than a town, it's a whole country. I'm supposed to be the Prime Minister. You're supposed to be the Foreign Secretary or something —— '

'Yes sir,' said Liz with grave, mock obedience.

'I think about it for hours. Sometimes I think, if we were married, and living somewhere in that house in the country, we could just sit and imagine ourselves there —— '

'By a log fire,' said Liz softly. 'And the fir trees all around, and no other house for miles.'

I looked at her squarely. She was as excited as I was in her own settled way. I was tossing a coin in my head, teetering on a decision. Heads I tell her, tails I don't. Heads I tell her this last thing.

'I want a room, in the house, with a green baize door,' I began calmly. 'It will be a big room, and when we pass into it, through the door, that's it, that's Ambrosia. No one else would be allowed in. No one else will have keys. They won't know where the room is. Only we will know. We'll make models of the principal cities, you know, out of cardboard, and we could use toy soldiers, painted, for the people. We could draw maps. It would be a place to go on a rainy afternoon. We could go there. No one would find us. I thought we would have a big sloping shelf running all the way down one wall, you know, like a big desk. And we'd have a lot of blank paper on it and design our own newspapers. We could even make uniforms, if we wanted to. It would be our country.' I stopped, suddenly aware of the cold and the black, peeling branches round about us and the ticking quiet of it all. I had talked myself right through the moment of contact. Liz, her old self, was grinning, pleased with life, seeing it all as our old fantasy, a kind of mental romp in the long grass. 'And let's have a model train, that the kids won't be allowed to use,' she said. 'And a big trench in the garden.'

I sank back, spreadeagling my hands in the grass to rid them of the webbed sensation that was coming back into them like a nervous tic.

'Liz,' I said, all the thoughts exhausted in me. 'Will you marry me?'

She leaned over me and whispered: 'Tomorrow,' in a throaty way. I pulled her down with a feeling of peace and misery, running my hands heavily down her back. She began to kiss me, not knowing that my eyes were open and staring. Her body was warm under the suède jacket and I found some kind of comfort, losing myself, not allowing anything into my head, but sinking into a kind of numb passion. Soon the whole incident had passed into history, to be exhumed and dissected soon, but not now. I felt the black dusty skirt give way as she fumbled at the zipper. I brushed my fingers against the smooth surface of her stomach, feeling her contract gingerly under the touch of them. She rolled over on to her back and I fell on top of her, grateful and easy in my mind, lost in her soft ways.

In the moment of satisfaction I said: 'There's somebody watching us.' From the bushes there was the sharp crack of breaking twigs and a resounding: 'Tskkkkkkkkk!'

I called: 'Whoever's out there is going to get their bastard teeth knocked down their throat in a minute!'

I scrambled to my feet, gathering my clothes about me like an Arab. Three youths leaped up from behind the bushes and began to run out of the woods, shouting directions at each other. Two of them were the youths who had been turned away from the Roxy, while I waited for Liz; the third was Stamp. I raced after them almost as far as the road. Stamp, stumbling drunkenly through the ferns, called in a falsetto voice: 'Oh, darling ——,' repeating some words I happened to have used a few minutes earlier. I let them go. As if it were far away, I heard Stamp call: 'Can I draw your maps for you, to play with?'

I walked back to the green grass, tucking my shirt into my trousers. Liz was sitting up and combing her hair. 'We should've stayed on the dance floor and let everybody have a look,' she said carelessly.

The idea, fanciful to her, made me go hot all over. Then I shivered. 'Let's go,' I said.

We began to walk back towards the Roxy. 'I'll wrap his cowing posters round his neck, next time I see him,' I said. But the idea of ever seeing Stamp again, or indeed anybody, filled me with horror.

Chapter Twelve

There was no sense in going back into the Roxy, and so I waited outside while Liz went in to fetch her handbag. It was getting late now, anyway. The commissionaire had changed into civilian clothes and was taking in the sandwich-boards and propping them against the wall inside the foyer. I could hear the Rockets playing tinnily inside, underlined by a steady thump-thump like a ship's engine. After the music there was some announcement over the tannoy which I could not hear. Mist' William Fisher, wanted on the telephone, no doubt; I wondered who had been ringing up for me at the Roxy and why. An inch of white ash fell from my cigarette. I began to walk up and down the parade of shops that lined the Roxy, staring at the gaunt, old-fashioned heads in the window of Molly, hair-stylist, and at the forlorn-looking estate agent's with its little cards buckling in their grained wooden slots. None of the shops looked as though anything had ever happened in them.

I had an instinct that I sometimes used, looking into the future and deciding whether an event would take place or not. I tried to project myself forward, to see whether Liz would come out again. I could not form any definite picture of her coming out and smiling at me, and I concluded that on the whole she would not. I decided to give her five more minutes, counting them off in sixties and folding a finger back for every minute gone. At the third finger I lost count over a commotion behind me. I turned round to see Stamp and his two idiot friends, reeling back from the Houghtondale Arms. Stamp was even drunker than he had been before, and was shouting at the top of his voice: *'To the woods! No, no, not the woods, anything but the woods!'* I stepped back into the estate agent's doorway. The commissionaire had gone round the back of the building with a coke shovel in his hand, and the Roxy was unguarded. They dodged in, giggling and shoving each other. 'Where's yer pass-outs, you two?' yelled Stamp. 'Hey, mister, they're getting in for nix!'

I was dog-tired and feeling gritty round the eyes, and hungry. I walked up to the entrance of the Roxy and looked down the length of the foyer, but I could not see Liz. She was probably already whooping it up with Man o' the Dales inside. At the door of the Ladies, Stamp was talking beerily to Rita, lending her a penny or something. I was hungry and cold and tired.

I walked away, dipping into my mind for a morsel of No. 1 thinking to get me home. Ambrosia was closed for the night, or seemed to be. I came up as chairman of the Stradhoughton Labour Party, in fact M.P. for the division, the youngest member in the House, writing letters to Councillor Duxbury. *Dear Councillor Duxbury, As you know, the proposal to nationalise the undertaking business is already in the committee stage. You are well versed not only in this particular field but in public life also, and before concluding this piece of legislation we would greatly appreciate your comments.* (*You may remember me as a clerk in your employ, many years ago now . . .*)

At the corner of Clogiron Lane was a fish shop, a small area of brightness among the discreet drawn blinds and the concrete lamps. I stepped almost automatically over the hollowed step into this tiled, light womb of warmth, and joined the small queue among the Tizer bottles, the stacked sheets of clean newspaper and the advertisements for cinemas and jumble sales. I leaned in gratitude on the salty marble counter and savoured the high aroma of steam and vinegar and buxom sweat. Written in whitewash on the burnished battery of mirrors above the frying-range was the sign: 'Under completely new management.' The usual fat women were serving in their chip-stained white aprons, but the man at the range, tall and dour like all fish shop proprietors, was a new one. He turned half-round to the trough of batter by his side, and I recognised him instantly as the leading man in an old No. 2 daymare which even now I revived from time to time. Long ago, in a different neighbourhood, I had caused some consternation up and down the street by telling everybody that the man who ran the fish shop had hanged himself. This was undoubtedly the same man. He recognised me too, and gave me one of the keen, contemplative looks that were so much a feature of Stradhoughton life. I had a quick fancy that all my enemies had secretly taken office around Clogiron Lane and were hustling into position, preparing for the coup. I bought my bag of chips and walked out of the shop.

Dear Mr Shadrack, As you know, the nationalisation of the undertaking business is imminent, and we are very keen to get someone knowledgeable in charge of casket production. I well remember as an 'old boy' of Shadrack and Duxbury's (I was the wretch who forgot to post the calendars!!!) being shown some drawings of a fibreglass casket which you thought could be produced very cheaply . . .

The chips lasted me all the way home to Hillcrest. I threw the greasy bag into our own privet hedge, wiped my hands and lit a cigarette before going indoors. I felt a lot better.

The old man was in the lounge, straddling the fawn tiled fireplace, the back of his balding head glimmering faintly through what little of the mirror you could see behind its crust of frosted bambis. His certificate of membership from the Ancient Order of Stags, thick with Gothic writing and seals and all the rest of it, was propped up on the mantelpiece. I was surprised to see the old man still up. He stood with his waist-coat open and eyed me as I went into the room.

I said: 'Did you want some chips bringing in?'

The old man said: 'I'm surprised t' bloody chip shop's still open, this time o' night.' He nodded towards the cuckoo clock, swinging its lead weights against the sad wallpaper. He turned to chuck his cigarette end in the fire and said, tossing the remark casually across to me: 'They're down at t' Infirmary.

'Who is?'

'Your mother and your grandma, who the bloody hell do you think? Your grandma's been taken badly again. We've been trying to get word to you for t' last hour. Where've you been?'

I felt a twinge of alarm at the idea of Gran being carted off to the Infirmary. Normally, after one of her fits, she would sit ticking broodily in a chair until she was more or less normal again. If the fit recurred, it was supposed to be serious or something. I was glad that they had got her out of the house.

I said, harshening my voice to make it acceptable: 'Why, what's up with her?'

'What's up wi' *you*, that's what I want to know,' the old

man snarled, beginning to boil up into his slow rage. 'I thought you were off to t' bloody dance hall when you'd been to t' pub. Why don't you go where you say you're going, we've been ringing up half the bloody night.'

'I had a pass-out —— ' I began.

'Pass-out, you'll do more than pass out if you don't bloody frame! You'd better ring up for a taxi, your mother wants to see you down at t' Infirmary.'

'Why, what's up wi' me grandma?' I said.

'What's allus up wi' your grandma, what do you think? Get ringing up t' taxi!'

Reluctantly, I went into the hall and rang up New Line Taxis. The old man was shouting: 'And bloody come home on a night in future, not at this bloody time!' but there was something oddly restrained and preoccupied about his abuse. I felt that he had something more to say. I put down the telephone and started to walk up the stairs. That was the trigger for it. With a bound of fury the old man reached the hall door.

'You don't go up there!'

'Why, I'm just waiting for t' taxi.'

'I said you don't go up there!'

I leaned against the wall, trying to look resigned and reasonable. 'Well ah've got to have a wash, haven't I?'

'You can go mucky. You don't go up*stairs*. We've had enough of you up there, with your bloody hiding and meddling and I don't know what else.'

'What, I don't know what you're talking about,' I said, screwing my face up to look puzzled.

'You know bloody well what I'm talking about.' And then, sharply: 'What have you done with that letter of your mother's?'

I stood, cold, on the stairs.

'Do you hear me? I'm talking to you!'

'What letter?' I said.

'What, what, what,' the old man mimicked, his face cracking into an ugly sneer. 'Don't keep saying bloody what! You know bloody well what letter! That what she gave you to post to t' Housewives' Choice.'

I leaned back again, my face in a mask of panic, reviewing breakneck all the things they must know if they had found out about my mother's letter.

'I've *told* her once, I posted it,' I said.

'You posted bloody nowt! You've had it in that box! It was given to you to post, you bloody, idle little bastard!'

A small wave of relief touched me, at the hope that the old man would put it all down to nothing more than idleness. I said, with desperate nonchalance: 'I *did* post it. That was just the rough copy.'

'What yer talking about, rough copy? It's your mother's letter. How *could* you have posted it?'

I came down one stair to meet him, trying to talk in the patient, explanatory voice. 'Look. The letter my mother wrote was full of mis*takes*, that's all. I just thought it would have a better chance if I wrote it out *again*, properly, that's all.'

'Well who told you to write it out again? And who told you to open it? You keep your thieving hands off other people's things! And where did you get all them bloody calendars from, anall?'

'What calendars?' It was a purely automatic reflex, like kicking up the knee against a hammer. I was trapped without time to think or to stall or to rig the facts.

The old man took a deep breath and started fingering the shredding, concave belt around his trousers. 'By bloody hell, I'll give you bloody what if you don't stop saying what, what, my lad! You know bloody well what! Don't think I've not been talking to Councillor Duxbury, cos I have! I've heard it all. You make me a bloody laughing-stock, you can't keep your hands off owt. And where's that monkey-wrench out of my garage? I suppose you know nowt about *that*?'

'No, course I don't. What do *I* want with a monkey-wrench?'

'What do you want wi' two hundred bloody calendars? And what have you been doing wi' their bloody nameplates anall? You're not right in the bloody head!'

I had no refuge except in rage. '*I'm* not right, *I'm* not right,' I shouted, coming down the stairs at him. '*I* didn't want to work for Shadrack and flaming Duxbury's. You put me there, now you can answer for it!'

'Don't bloody shout at me, you gormless young get! Or I'll knock your bloody eyes out.'

'God give me strength,' I murmured, closing my eyes at the threat.

'God give you strength, he wants to give you some bloody sense! You're like a bloody Mary Ann!' He was slowing down, like a spent volcano. I sat down on the stairs with my head in my hands, trying to look defeated and hoping he would go away. He turned, muttering to himself. 'Well I hope yer mother gets more sense out o' you. And don't go chelping back at her like you chelp at me, else you'll know about it.' He stood at the hall door, fingering the lock, experimenting with the turning mechanism, and trying hard to effect the transition from shouting into normal speech. I tried to help him.

'Well I *told* you I didn't want to work for Shadrack's when I first started, didn't I?'

'You didn't want to work for nobody, if you ask me owt,' the old man said. 'You thought you'd live on me, didn't you?'

'No, I didn't. I could have kept myself.'

'How?'

'Writing scripts,' I said thickly.

'Writing bloody scripts, you want to get a day's work done, never mind writing scripts. Who do you think's going to run *this* bloody business when *I'm* gone?' He jerked his thumb in the direction of the garage outside, and it was so exactly like the trouble at t' mill routine that Arthur and I had between us that the response flicked immediately into my mind: *'But father, we all have our lives to lead, you yours and I mine!'*

Aloud, I said: 'You said you didn't *want* me in the business.'

'Only because you were so bloody idle! *Some* bastard's got to carry on wi' it. Who's going to keep your mother?'

Father, the men! They're coming up the drive!

'Why, you're not retiring, are you?' I said with a forced jocularity. The old man turned away in disgust and walked into the lounge. I sat where I was for a minute or so, and then I started to go upstairs. 'And keep out of your grandma's bedroom!' he called venomously.

I tiptoed into my room and went straight over to the Guilt Chest, already convinced that the whole thing had been a gigantic hoax. But the chest had definitely been moved; it was lying slantwise across the linoleum, only half-under the bed, and the stamp edging was gone. It was almost a relief to know at last for certain that they had been into it. I knelt down and pulled the Guilt Chest clear of the bed and lifted the tinny lid. The calendars were still stacked in their heavy piles, though they had been disturbed. The Housewives' Choice letter had gone. I felt under a pile of calendars for the stack of invoices the old man had once given me to post. They were still there. I grabbed them first, the calendars toppling over into the chest, and stuffed them into my inside pocket. Liz's postcards were still there, and so was the copy of Ritzy Stories. The letters from the Witch had been interfered with. I ran rapidly through their contents and turned the repeater gun on the Witch and her silly, daft prose.

I sat on the bed, making a weak effort to translate the scene with the old man into No. 1 thinking, with my No. 1 father ushering me into the library for the manly talk. I tried again to project myself into the future. I could see myself, quite plainly see myself, sitting on the train, knocking on a peeling door in Earl's Court, sitting in Danny Boon's office, eating beans on toast in the A.B.C. I took out my wallet and counted the notes again, eight pounds ten now, and seventeen shillings in silver.

I dug out the letter from Danny Boon again and smoothed it out and read it. '*Several of the boys do work for me, you might be interested in this.*' I jumped to my feet and grabbed the old suitcase from under the chest of drawers, throwing out the store of blankets and Polythene-wrapped cardigans my mother kept in it. Pulling open drawers, I began to assemble shirts and handkerchiefs and socks together. I took down my best suit and folded it in two, still on its hanger, inside the suitcase. Then I looked in the Guilt Chest, reckoning that there must be about a hundred and seventy calendars left. I got a great heap of calendars and put them, in three rows, in the suitcase. Then I began packing in earnest, putting a calendar in between each shirt and placing the calendars like lining all the way round the case. The lid would not close. I took out two shirts and one calendar. I tore the calendar out of its envelope and propped it up on the bedroom mantelpiece behind the Coronation tin. I pushed the envelope behind the sheet of newspaper in the fireplace, and got the case shut by pressing on it. There was a rubble of old letters and torn pieces of envelope left in the Guilt Chest. I put Liz's postcards and the letters from the Witch in my raincoat pocket, and left the rest.

I was humming as I went into the bathroom to fetch my toothbrush.

The old man shouted up the stairs: 'Do you hear? T' taxi's come!'

I shouted: 'All right! Just coming,' and put out the light.

Chapter Thirteen

The old man did not see the suitcase, and so there was no trouble in getting out of the house. The taxi driver was one we knew slightly, a man who sometimes came round to Hillcrest to help on jobs. I leaned back against the spent and slithery leather-work, pretending he was a stranger. I clicked without real interest into the piece of No. 1 thinking I always reserved for taxis; my chauffeur-driven Bentley running through the home counties and stopping at the prosperous, half-timbered pub. 'Have you eaten, Benson? Better put the car round the back and join me, hadn't you?'

'What's up, then?' said the real taxi-driver as we turned into Clogiron Lane. 'Is somebody poorly?'

'Yer, me grandma,' I said. 'She's had one o' them turns again.'

'Well, you can expect it, can't yer? She's not getting any younger.'

'No.'

'She's a grand old lass, though, i'n't she?'

'Yer.'

Stradhoughton Infirmary was a white Portland stone building, rusting round the window-sills and mottled with the bleaching it had had from the so-called brackish air. In the light of the concrete lamps it looked even more like a madhouse than ever. We pulled up outside the scratched swing doors and I told the taxi to wait. I took the suitcase in with me. I was met by the dead smell of lavender polish; it was like breathing through a furry yellow duster. The portraits of aldermen and benefactors looked down over the deserted central hall. I went through the white door into the casualty department.

It was busy in its late-night, sleep-walking way. On the high-backed benches a knot of women were joined in a litany of bad doctors, inadequate pensions and leaky houses. They whiled away the time indignantly while their husbands had emergency operations or their children suffered. They were the same women, or seemed to be the same women, I had seen earlier in the New House, the ones who knew about life and death and all the rest of it. I no longer envied them. A man with his arm in a sling sat alone and perplexed, wondering why he had come. He was the one I warmed to. Over by the ambulance bay the porters looked as though they did not care about anything, sitting in their little glass office smoking Woodbines crooked in the hollow of their hands. They distended their necks and frowned and altered their mouths into an oblong shape to expel the smoke. A young char in spectacles swilled at the parquet floor. Nurses in white and purple held huddled conferences that were not to do with the dying. The women talked: 'He put me on port wine.'

I found my mother sitting alone in the corridor on a padded bench that had been ripped and sawed at with a knife until the grey stuffing spilled out like brains. I put down the suitcase and went over and stood in front of her. She looked up.

'We looked all over,' she said weakly, and cleared her throat.

'Where's me grandma?'

She nodded towards the flapping doors where the corridor came to an end. 'They've got that black doctor to her. She can't talk. We're just waiting.' She spoke hoarsely, in a resigned way, yet at the same time excitedly. These were the headlines. I knew, for I had seen her lips moving, that she was already rehearsing the text of this eventful day, plucking at the details of it like pomegranate seeds and stringing them together in a long rosary that would be fingered on and off long after anyone had ceased to care. 'We've been trying to get you since half-past nine,' she said. 'I wanted you to come down with me.'

'I know, my dad was saying,' I said, trying to sound like his son. 'He says she's badly this time.'

My mother sucked in her cheeks and moistened her tongue ready for the first run of her long narrative.

'She was all right again at four o'clock, just after you went out,' she began. 'She had a cup of tea at half-past, when we had ours, but she wouldn't have any brown bread. Then she had a sleep. And she was all right at *nine* o'clock, when your father got back from the pub, because she woke up and asked him if he were putting t' television on. Then we were all just sitting watching television —— ' (later she would add the name of the programme and of the singer and possibly of the song) – 'when she just slumped forward in her chair. We thought she were having a fit, but no, she just gave a little jerk with her head, uh, like that there' – she imitated the jerk, and searched with her magpie memory to see if there was some pin she had left unaccounted for in the first five minutes of my grandmother's dying. 'Then she started to slaver. She were just like a baby. It was pitiful, pitiful. Just like a baby, slavering and gasping for breath.

'Anyway, your father said, if it isn't a fit, we'd better ring for Dr *Mor*gan. So we waited five more minutes and she was still slavering, she wet four handkerchiefs through, them big handkerchiefs of your dad's, so I said you'd better ring up and get t' doctor.'

The account droned on until we had covered every paving-stone on the way to the Infirmary. I was not listening but I knew all that she was saying; I responded, Mm, Mm, Mm, at every pause. I did not want the details of it, not every detail, and I began concentrating on objects in the corridor and thinking the wall, the wall, the ceiling, the ceiling, so that the things my mother was saying could ricochet off them and lose what force they had.

'The last thing she said before they got her on t' stretcher was Where's my Jack. I had to think who she was talking about, then I remembered she must have meant your grandad. Only she always used to call him John. She *ne*ver called him Jack, never. Then she said, *I love you, Jack*' – my mother had difficulty in pronouncing this word love. I had never heard her say it before, and it sounded strange on her lips. I tried to imagine it on the lips of the yellow woman on the other side of the swing doors, but it was impossible. I – love – you. My mother said it as though the word had just been invented, like Terylene.

'Oh, before that she said, What are you thinking about. I think she must ha' been talking to your grandad.' My mother stopped and took a long breath, the breath coming out in a staircase of sighing. 'But you had to listen close to, to hear what she was saying. She could hardly speak, and by the time we got here she couldn't speak at all. She was just slavering.'

She seemed to have finished. I had been trying on various expressions and by now I was searching feverishly for one that really belonged to me. I found it difficult to feel anything beyond indignation that my grandmother should be seen off with this gossiping commentary. Even as my mother was speaking, the phrases with which Arthur and I dissected the conversations around us kept slotting into my head like price tabs ringing up on a cash register. 'Never use a preposition to end a sentence with.' 'I must ask you to not split infinitives.' I felt disgust at myself but when I shopped around for some deeper emotion, there was none. I had a nervous urge to laugh, and I found myself concentrating entirely on keeping my face adult and sad.

My mother said: 'They're a long time.' I had no idea how long she had been here, in spite of the time-table she had given me. She stirred on the creaking couch and seemed to shake herself free of her drama. She turned to me, seeing me probably for the first time as her son and not only as a listener.

'Well, you've got yourself into a fine mess, lad, haven't you?' she said.

I got up and stretched, elaborately, turning away from her. 'So it would seem.'

'I'm only thankful *she* knows nowt about it,' my mother said. She was silent for a minute or so. It seemed to me that she did not want to discuss the subject but was pushing herself into it.

'Why didn't you post that letter of mine?'

'I *did* post it. I was telling me dad. I just wrote it out again, that's all.' I had been working on the story since leaving the old man and got it into convincible shape, but I was tired and it no longer seemed to matter.

'What did you want to write it out again for?'

'There were some mistakes in it. I just thought it would stand a better chance if it was better written, that's all.' I was beginning to feel annoyed with her for picking at trivialities at a time like this.

'Yes, well we can't all be Shakespeares, can we,' she said, in a way that was supposed to shame me. She glanced down the corridor at my suitcase against the wall. She showed no surprise, and I knew that she must have noticed it already and decided to say nothing.

'And what have you been saying to Arthur's mother about having a sister?' she said in sharper tones.

'Why, it was only a joke,' I said, not even bothering to try and sound convincing. I did not know how she knew about Arthur's mother, and I did not care.

'A joke, it *sounds* like a joke. And I thought you told me she'd broken her leg?'

'I didn't know you *knew* Arthur's mother,' I said.

'Yes, you don't know who I know and who I don't know, do you? If you want to know, she rang me up. And what did you do with that cardigan she gave you?'

I remembered this. Arthur's mother had once given me a red cardigan for my imaginary sister. I had carted it around town all day and then left it on a bus.

'Gave it to Barbara, thought I told you about it,' I said.

'You tell me nothing. You didn't tell me about giving her cheek outside t' cemetery this afternoon, did you? When you were *with* Barbara. Anyway, she's coming round tomorrow, when Barbara comes for her tea. So you've got a new cardigan to find.'

I decided to speak. She had seen the suitcase, so she knew, but I decided to tell her.

'I won't be here tomorrow,' I said.

My mother sat bolt upright and pursed her lips, pulling in any expression she might have had on her face. She could not disguise a look of restrained shock, as though I had suddenly struck her and she was trying not to show it.

'I'd have gone already if it hadn't been for me grandma,' I said, as gently as I could.

She looked at me, a long, sorrowing look. 'If you're in trouble, Billy, it's not something you can leave behind you, you know,' she said in a shaky voice. 'You put it in your suitcase and take it with you.'

My mother was so little given to this kind of imagery that I wondered if she had got rush reports on the calendars in my suitcase.

'Well I'm still going,' I said doggedly. 'I told you I'm going and I'm going.'

The swing doors opened softly. A nurse came padding along the corridor, walking like an actress. She stopped by my mother and said: 'Mrs Fisher?' in the tones of somebody trying to wake somebody else up from sleep. '*Would* you come this way?' Infected by the mood of feigned solicitude, I stood up as my mother, the light of fear in her eyes, rose and walked slowly with the nurse through the swing doors. I sat down, suddenly tense and frightened. I said to myself, clenching my fists, Don't let's have any scenes, don't let's have any scenes, don't let's have any scenes. I wondered rapidly whether to go now, but I knew I would not. I began pawing the floor with embarrassment. I picked up an old newspaper that had been shoved down the back of the bench, and began to read aimlessly. *'Three passengers on a Belfast plane recently were Mr GOOSE, Mr GANDER and the Rev Mr GOSLING. They did not know each other.'* Beneath this news item was a cartoon, of a little boy saying: 'Can I see this gab that daddy says you have the gift of, Mrs Jones?' I chucked the paper down and began walking from one side of the corridor to the other, heel to toe as though measuring out a cricket pitch. Don't let's have any *scenes*.

It was only a few minutes before my mother came back, holding her handbag between her hands, her face marked with grief and dignity as she imagined it to be. She was helped as far as the doors by a grave-faced doctor, and it looked to me like some corny act on television. I could not help these thoughts. I prayed: please, God, let me *feel* something. Let me feel something, only don't let's have any scenes.

'Your grandma died at fourteen minutes past twelve,' my mother said, as though making a formal announcement. I wanted to say: 'I'm sorry' or something, but anything I said would have sounded ridiculous. 'I shall have to sit down,' my mother said. I sat by her, legs apart, head bowed, staring down at my feet and counting the stains on my suede shoes. I examined what I was feeling and it was nothing, nothing.

My mother was already in the luxury of reminiscing. 'She would have wanted it this way,' she said, a platitude so inept that I could only marvel at the clichés that she used like crutches to take her limping from one crisis to another. And at the same time I was relieved to hear her talk like this; I thought, They're as bad as I am, they don't feel it, they only say it. But I did not believe what I was telling myself.

'Do you want to go in and see her?' my mother said. I mumbled 'No,' mingling shock and shame.

She sighed, drawing on her gloves. 'Well, we'll have to carry on as best we can,' she said. She stared at the wall, moving her lips again. 'Her last words were just Jack, Jack, what are you thinking about.'

And she died with a slavered smile and not a genuine thought from anybody. No one had been capable of a genuine thought. All those women, who were supposed to know it all, all about life and death, they didn't know any more than I did.

'Can we get a cup of tea, I've had nothing to eat since half-past four,' my mother said.

'Yer, there's a canteen out in the waiting-room,' I mumbled. I hovered about, pretending to help her up, and we walked down the corridor.

'We shall have to ring up Mr Shadrack,' my mother said. I had been fearing this, ever since I had heard that Gran was ill, and often in the past I had worked out how to get out of it if they ever wanted a Shadrack and Duxbury funeral for her.

'You don't want to get them, you want to get the Co-op,' I said.

My mother, speaking as though she was ashamed, said: 'Why, do they pay a divi?' and it was as though her voice was being pulled back on a lead, like a dog.

I said: 'No, but they're better than blinking Shadrack and Duxbury's.'

We were back in the hall of the casualty department. The canteen was still open. I went over to the steamy aluminium-ridged counter with the pale milky rings on it, and ordered sloppy tea in a thick mug marked SGI, Stradhoughton General Infirmary. I took the cup over to my mother and then went back and fetched my suitcase. I stood it almost in front of her and sat down. All the women had gone. There was only an old tramp in a dirty raincoat, his foot bandaged, sitting like a lost man in the corner.

My mother put her cup on the floor, shaking her head. 'I can't drink it.' She twisted her wedding ring.

'What train are you supposed to be catching?' she said.

'I don't know, when there is one.' And then, in the gentle voice: 'I've *got* to go tonight, because I want to see Danny Boon on Monday morning.'

My mother opened her handbag. 'Well you haven't got any money, have you?'

I said, flushing for the first time: 'I've got a few pounds.

I've been saving up.' I was beginning to get embarrassed. I wanted to be away and finished with it all. I said: 'You'd better be getting back. I've got a taxi waiting for you outside.'

'I've got some papers to sign first,' my mother said. She stared down at the cup of tea on the floor. 'We don't say much,' she said – a straight lie, for a start – 'but we need you at home, lad.'

The sudden editorial 'we' made me feel uncomfortable. 'Well, I'll be coming home,' I said. With a rush of generosity I added: 'I'll just get fixed up with Danny Boon and then I'll come home next week-end.'

She shook her head slightly from side to side, saying nothing.

'Well I'll *have* to go, because I don't know what time the train is,' I said. 'T' taxi's just outside, when you're ready.' I shuffled about in front of her, trying to say some words that I had practised for this moment, but I could not say them. I walked away slowly, trying to look as though I were reluctant to go. By the time I reached the white door I was already thinking of Gran as an article in the *Reader's Digest*. *'Ma Boothroyd said what she thought. Everyone feared her blunt tongue. Came the day when Ma Boothroyd had to go to hospital . . .'* Twenty-three, twenty-four, twenty-five. The Lord is my shepherd, I shall not want, he maketh me to lie down in green pastures.

I did not have the courage to turn round and look at my mother, but I knew that her face would be flawed and crumpled like an old balloon, and that for the first time she would be looking as though these things had really happened.

Chapter Fourteen

The strange, poppy-like flowers seen nowhere else in the world were in full bloom in Ambrosia, or what was left of it. We had won the elections, and I was pressing forward with my visionary plan to build an entire city over the dunes on a gigantic wooden platform. The reactionary Dr Grover had got a commission set up to investigate me, but I knew for a fact that he had been bribed to put forward a rival plan for another city to the west, over the marshes. In the inner layers of No. 1 thinking, Grover got his way and the houses began to sink, seventy-one dead and fourteen unaccounted for. 'We will rebuild,' I announced in the *Ambrosia Poppy*. 'We will build on the dunes.' Now I was home on a visit to my parents, my full-dress uniform unbuttoned at the throat. The telephone rang, and I spoke rapidly in Ambrosian to one of my lieutenants. *'Monay. D'cra d'njin, intomr nay nay Grover. D'cra Grover, n'jnin repost. Finis.'* My mother was impressed, but no, she was not impressed. How could she be, that one? I tried to fit in my No. 1 mother, but she was a piece from another jigsaw. I began to slide off into some hate thinking about my real mother and her clichés and her knitting, about my dead grandmother snickering 'Good night' at the television set and the old man, stolid and daft, pulling his faces and banging nails all over the garage. *'Dad, I shall want the van. Don't ask questions. There may be people here. You don't know where I've gone or when I'm coming back. O.K.?'* I was sick and tired of it all, of it all.

I walked with my suitcase, following the pitch-pocked channels in the road where the tramlines had been. I was beginning to feel like a man made entirely of sawdust. I tried to get back to Ambrosia but none of it would click and I had nothing but hate for anybody. I fired off the repeater gun at all the people who knew my secrets, but none of the secrets really mattered, they were like dead wounds with the bandages falling off. I started to get clear, frightening thoughts. Nine pounds. Less the fare, call it seven. Seven pounds. If I can get a room for two pounds ten a week, that's two weeks and a quid a week for food. I can always get a job of some kind, maybe washing-up. I began to imagine myself in the tradition of American writers, driving lorries, sweeping up, South American revolution, soda jerk, newspaper boy. Then the No. 1 thinking switched off, this time at the mains. I knew that it would probably be a job as a clerk, in an office, but by myself, by myself. No Stamps, no Shadracks. I could be an eccentric. The surly one, the man with the past.

Saturday night was over and done with. Along Infirmary Street a low wind caught and held a sheet of brown paper and wrapped it round a lamp-post. I could hear cars whining up Houghtondale Hill two miles away. One or two rashly-hired taxis, piled high with people splitting the fare, ran past me on their way to the Strad Lee housing estate, and I caught the idiot murmur of their radios instructing the drivers as they passed. The late bus went by, looking as though it was the last bus that would ever run again anywhere, its occupants reading the *Empire News* under the blue glare. A dog padded across the road. A man stamped home in his raincoat and I knew that he was counting the lamp-posts to get there quicker. The pavement was dry and hollow, here and there etched with the trickle of long-stale urine. The streets were cold and the girls on the posters were grinning in their sleep.

I walked like a ghost down Moorgate, the suitcase making red ridges on my hand and turning into loot at every sight of a policeman. I turned into Bull Ring, dodging the slow-moving road-sweeper vans emerging like snails from the cleansing department and leaving their trickling smear along the gutters. I walked across Bull Ring into New Station.

The station was ablaze with cold, white light. The booking hall was deserted except for a fleet of electric trollies piled high with newspaper parcels. The last Harrogate diesel was just pulling sleekly away from platform two.

The enquiry office was closed. I walked up to the roller indicator where the trains were listed: 1.05 Wakefield, Doncaster; 1.35 Leeds (City), Derby, Kettering, London (St Pancras); 1.50 Selby, Market Weighton, Bridlington, Filey, Scarborough. There were no other trains to London that night. All the windows but one at the ticket office were boarded up. I waited under A-G until a tired man in his shirt-sleeves appeared, and I bought a single second-class to St Pancras. It cost thirty-five shillings. I looked up at the big station clock. It was ten minutes to one.

Below the ticket office was the buffet and main waiting-room. The buffet end was closed, its counter still lined with thick cups and the floor littered with crusts of bread, but there were about a dozen people still in the waiting-room, most of them asleep with their feet up on the scratched tubular chairs or their heads down on the rockety tables, among the flattened straws and empty lemon-squash cartons. I went in and stood by the door, under one of the large, empty-looking pictures of fields and hills that lined the walls. A few people were awake: half a dozen soldiers, all in civvies, going home on leave, three old prostitutes, a man in a large black coat. I was sleepy, recognising everything about five seconds after it happened. I did not see Rita, or Stamp, until I had settled down on my suitcase and was lighting a cigarette.

They did not see me either. Stamp, savouring the dregs of his dull, drunken evening, was leaning against one of the gilded pillars that separated the waiting-room from the buffet, sweating and muttering to himself. Rita was pulling ineffectually at his arm, like a tired wife trying to get her husband out of the pub. '*Come* on, they're all *looking* at you,' I heard her say impatiently. She stood indecisively and then let go of his arm and said, obviously not for the first time: 'Oh, well I'm going, you can look after yourself.' Stamp, lost in the biley swamps of his own suffering, gripped the pillar for support and comfort, retched, swallowed and then, in his thin and watery way, was sick all over the floor. Rita tutted and phewed and looked rapidly from side to side to find sympathy for her own predicament. She walked a few steps away and turned her back, standing with a formal casualness, pretending not to be anything to do with Stamp. A few of the sleeping people stirred. One of them half-awoke.

'Christ sake, shift outside if you wanna spew!'

Some of those who were already awake began tittering. One of the soldiers imitated a man in the toils of sickness. *'Wyyach!'* Stamp, clawing at the air, reeling and watery-eyed, caught some kind of hazy glimpse of me sitting in the corner, watching him. The image passed straight though into his subconscious and he peered at me without recognition, fixing his eyes on me only as an object while he strained and sweated and gasped for air.

The man in the big black coat, red-faced and beery in his own right, was enjoying it all. For the benefit of the soldiers he called: 'Get that man in the guard-house! C.O.'s prade, morrow morning. Hat off, left right left right left right HALT!' One or two of the soldiers grinned weakly; the one sitting next to me muttered: 'He wants to get back in the blasted army if he's so blasted keen.'

Stamp, mopping grimily at his damp forehead, staggered to the wall and sat down on the floor under a picture of Lake Windermere, head down like a sleeping Mexican. Rita walked over and began plucking at him again, pleading: '*Come* on, then. You shouldn't drink and then you wouldn't *be* like this.'

In the middle of the room, the tableau changed. The three old prostitutes were haggling with a half-drunk, fair-haired lad who had just come in. 'Well do you want *her*, then? You should have said. *She* doesn't care, one way or t' other.' They were all about fifty years old, and they did not look like prostitutes, more like housewives who baked loaves. They talked like mothers anxious to please their grown-up sons with a good tea. 'Well get a taxi and take her home then. She'll take fifteen shillings, she doesn't care, she doesn't want to skin you.'

The soldiers next to me were muttering. '*He* must be hard up for it, they look like three old grandmothers.'

'Three old grandmothers, bet they'll be getting their pensions in the morning!'

'Ha! Be funny if one of 'em pegged out on the job. Three dirty old grandmothers.'

It was wit to the taste of Stamp, but Stamp saw nothing of what was going on around him. He had got up and was leaning over his pillar again, slavering into the thin green mess which he had padded about the floor with his sick-speckled shoes.

'Wyyach!' went one of the soldiers.

'That time me and Jacko got them German drinks. *Wyyach!*'

I got up and walked to the other side of the waiting-room, skirting round Stamp in a broad arc. As soon as Rita saw me I regretted that I had moved.

'Look what's crawled out of the cheese!' she said, neither raising nor lowering her voice. She was wearing a blue swagger coat over her tight red dress. The silver cross was no longer round her neck.

'I should think some people ought to crawl back *in*to the cheese,' I said, nodding towards Stamp.

'Oo, where's yer rubber halo?' jeered Rita. We looked at each other, or at least I looked at her. Rita had a habit of looking at nothing, her eyes glazing over with a sort of gormless preoccupation.

'What happened to the Witch?' I said.

She screwed her face up into an ugly scowl. *Who?'*

'Barbara. Her you were talking to in the Roxy.'

'Don't know, don't care,' said Rita.

'Did she say anything?'

'Ask no question and you'll get no lies told,' she said in the same level voice.

'I bet she got that cross out of you,' I said recklessly. 'Hope you didn't give her the ring back, did you?'

Rita's voice suddenly took on the same pitch and colour as the voices of the three old prostitutes still haggling away in the middle of the room:

'You what? Do you think I'm daft, or what? It might be her cross, but you gave that ring to *me*!'

I looked around, but nobody was listening.

'I know, only it's a bit of a mix-up,' I said. 'You see, I thought Barbara had broke the engagement off —— '

'Yer, well you've another think coming if you think I'm as daft as she is! You gave that ring to *me*, in front of a witness.'

'How do you mean, what's witnesses got to do with it?'

Rita stared at me, thin-lipped like all the people I had known that day. She made as if to speak twice and then, spitting the words out with such force that her head shook, she said in the lowest range of her coarse voice:

'You're just *rot*ten, aren't you?'

I looked wildly across the room to my suitcase, and from my suitcase to the door, planning the shortest route out into the booking hall.

'Y'are! You're rotten! All through! I've met some people in my time but of all the lying, scheming —— Anyway, you gave that ring to *me*!'

I said quietly and urgently: 'Look, nobody's asking for the ring. You can have it —— '

'Don't talk to me, you rotten get!' Rita's voice was rising with each word, and even the prostitutes were beginning to stare. 'Get back to *'er*! You rotten get! You rotten, lying get! Gar, you think you're summat, don't you? But you're nowt! You miserable, lying, rotten, stinking get!'

White-faced, I turned my back on her and walked quickly towards my suitcase, skidding and almost losing my balance where Stamp had been sick on the floor. 'You think you're it but you're spit!' shouted Rita. One of the soldiers caught my eye and jerked his head up, raising his eyes and going: 'Cuh!' I grabbed my suitcase blindly and made for the door. Two railway policemen walked into the waiting-room, looking ponderously about them, and Rita shut up. One of them walked over to where Stamp was leaning helplessly against the pillar and began talking to him in a low, dangerous voice.

The man in the black coat called: 'Two men, buckets, mops. Floor cleaned. Port to me when you've finished. Double!' I slid out of the waiting-room and stood irresolutely in the booking hall, still shaken.

It was just on one o'clock. I stood contemplating the gigantic advertisement for Ovaltine that filled one whole end of the booking hall. Running my eyes down the wall, I began to count the loaded parcel trolleys that stood around the station. I got up to nineteen, and then the waiting-room door opened again and one of the policemen came out, helping Stamp towards the lavatory. Stamp saw me with his boiled, steaming eyes and muttered through the spit on his face: 'Know somethn bou' you, Fisher. *I* saw you. Wai' Monday, you jus' wai'.' The policeman led him off, as he muttered again: 'Wai' Monday.'

I had lost my place among the parcel trolleys. I began counting the tiles on the dirty, unwashed floor of the station. I counted them in a line, screwing up my eyes, and numbering each tile only with great difficulty after I had passed twenty. Raising my head slightly I saw a pair of heels by the one window of the ticket office that was still open. I opened my eyes again and looked, and there was no mistaking the casual black skirt, the green suède jacket and the unkempt hair. Liz was just turning away from the ticket office as I picked up my case and began to stumble towards her, walking drunkenly in the manner of Stamp being led off to the lavatory.

She saw me just as she was turning off to make for the platform where the Doncaster train was waiting. I waved, and she came towards me. I flapped my hand again, airily.

'Goin' London,' I mumbled, grabbing her arm and lurching about in front of her. 'You goin' London? I'm goin' London. Go' catch a train. Goin' London.'

'So you keep saying,' said Liz, beaming comfortably.

'You come London, me. Goin' London. Pla'form three, S' Pancra', ge's all London.'

'Where did you get it?' said Liz, still beaming as though she relished the whole thing.

'Where ge' wha'?'

'The booze. Or did you find some little dive to go to after you so mysteriously disappeared?'

'Go' go London,' I said. 'Carn stay Stradanan. Go' go London.'

The station announcer, as inarticulate as myself, crackled out some message about the Doncaster train. Liz looked up at the station clock.

'Well *I'm* not going to London. I've got to go to Doncaster ——'

I took hold of her arm again, wagging my head heavily.

'No, you come London. Need you London. Ge' nother ticket, come London.'

Liz gave me one of her long looks, and slowly took hold of me, inspecting me at arm's length.

'Drop it,' she said, stern behind the smile.

I said in my normal voice: 'Drop what?'

'That's better. You may be a brilliant scriptwriter, Billy, but you're a rotten actor.'

I put on an elaborate mock-sheepish act, standing on one foot, pulling out a grin and spreading my arms about.

'*All* right,' said Liz. 'Now where did you get to tonight?'

'Where did *I* get to? Where did *you* get to?'

Lovingly, in detail, we reconstructed the half hour I had waited outside the Roxy, charting and justifying our movements, forgiving and understanding, and everything so simple. Liz had been having a long talk with the Witch, whom she had discovered weeping and slobbering and sick on the floor of the Ladies. Everything that could be told had been told.

'Are you really going to London, or just pretending?' said Liz.

I took the ticket out of my pocket and showed it to her.

She looked at me steadily and there was love in her dark eyes, the first time I had seen it, a liquid, far-reaching thing, too deep to touch.

'I'm not coming, you know, Billy.'

'Please.'

She shook her head. 'I won't live with you, Billy.'

'Come anyway,' I said. 'Live next door. Blimey, you've been everywhere else, you might as well come and live in —— ' I broke off as a suspicion crossed my mind. 'Why are you going to Doncaster?'

She grinned again, in the frank manner that gave nothing away.

'Oh, just – Doncaster,' she said, shrugging amiably.

I said bluffly, in the man of the world voice: 'Well whatever you want in Doncaster, they've got it in London. Yes? Yes?'

She was shaking her head, smiling.

'One condition,' she said.

I closed my eyes tightly and smote my forehead, teetering on the brink of a decision. All the details of it were there, in a compact parcel of No. 1 thinking, from the register office ceremony to the Chelsea attic. All it needed was the decision.

'And *I* wouldn't want the communal ring,' said Liz. But *I* did not answer, and she knew that there was no answer.

A porter was rattling the gate at the entrance to the Doncaster platform. Liz picked up her bag, a small, well-worn grip. She regarded me steadily for a few seconds and, standing a foot in front of me, blew me a kiss.

'Postcards?' she said, whispering it.

'Postcards,' I said.

I struck the farewell attitude, legs apart, arms akimbo, the sad figure fading into silhouette as the train steams away. But she did not look back. The porter banged the gate shut and I saw Liz clamber into the last carriage after two soldiers. I watched the train disappear. I knew that she would already be in bright conversation, grinning engagingly at some item of army news.

It was twelve minutes past one. I picked up my suitcase and walked back towards the waiting-room. Rita, the three old prostitutes and most of the others had gone, and there was sawdust on the floor where Stamp had been. Two soldiers slept on, their feet extended across a couple of chairs apiece. The man in the black coat was still there, but dozing.

I stood by the wall and, raising one leg, balanced the suitcase on my knee. I took out the top layer of calendars and began rooting about among the shirts and socks for more. I stacked the calendars on the tubular table beside me until I had got them all out. Then I closed the suitcase and pushed it under the table. I scooped the calendars up into two heavy parcels, one under each arm, and barged the door open with my back. I looked up and down the booking hall but there was nobody watching. There was a deep wire litter bin, labelled 'Keep Your Borough Clean'. I bent over and tipped the calendars into it. The basket toppled slightly. I gathered up some newspapers from a nearby seat and stuffed them in on top of the calendars.

I turned to go and then, struck by a second thought, I felt in my pocket for the wad of invoices that I should have posted for the old man. I dropped those in the basket too. I found the letters from the Witch, and ripped them in pieces, scattering the bits in the litter bin and on the floor around it. I began going methodically through my pockets, discarding practically everything: the fragment of script for Danny Boon, the letter I had started to write to him, a couple of Stamp's passion pills, a cigarette packet. When I had finished I had nothing left but the note from Danny Boon, Liz's postcards, and my railway ticket. I walked back into the waiting-room and got my suitcase. It needed fourteen minutes before the London train was due to go.

Ambrosia came softly into my head, the beginning of it all, with the march-past and the one-armed soldiers and the flags. I muttered to myself, almost aloud: 'Seventy-eight ninety-six, a hundred and four, the Lord is my Shepherd, I shall not want, he maketh me to lie down in green pastures, he leadeth me beside the still waters.' The No. 1 thinking fused into a panic-panorama with the No. 2 daymares and the quick sharp shafts of ordinary, level thought. I imagined myself as a modern clergyman, pipe-smoking, twinkling, arranging a contemporary funeral with Shadrack; but nasally he was saying, 'It's vair vair unsatisfactory, vair unsa'sfactory.' I could not summon up my No. 1 mother, only the real one, with her pressed, depressed mouth and her petty frown. Seven pounds, seven pounds ten actually, get a room for thirty bob a week, call it three weeks, three quid left, half a crown a day, egg and chips one and threepence, cup of tea threepence, bus fares a tanner. He restoreth my soul, he leadeth me in the paths of righteousness for his name's sake. I saw Liz in the Chelsea attic, and Rita whoring it in the streets outside, and the Witch as the reactionary Dr Grover's mistress. I tried hard to shut it down and find myself, myself, but not knowing what to do for characteristics. Yea, though I walk through the valley of the shadow of death, I will fear no evil.

The station announcer began to list the stations to London. Leeds (City), Derby, Kettering, London (St Pancras). Change at Leeds for Bradford, Ilkley, Bolton Abbey. The man in the big black coat, chastened now, began to arrange his things. I got up and began to walk hurriedly up and down the waiting-room; I had the sensation of a water-tap running in my stomach. I picked up my suitcase and put it down twice. I took out the ticket and looked at it, vaguely noting the price and the details. I could not think, except in confused snatches. I began to count ten; at the end of the count I would oblige myself to answer one way or the other. One. Two. Three. Four. The train now leaving platform three is the one thirty-five for London, calling at. Five. Six. Seven. There was no need to count to the end. I picked up the suitcase, feeling deflated and defeated. I walked out of the waiting-room and across the booking hall to the ticket barrier on platform three, hoping that I would make a quick decision but knowing that there was no question of it. The man in the black coat and three or four soldiers walked through, showing their tickets.

The ticket collector looked at me.

'You gettin' on this train?' I shook my head, taking a step forward at the same time.

I did not wait for the train to leave. I transferred the suitcase to my left hand and walked out of the station. In Bull Ring I stopped and lit a cigarette and buttoned up my coat. The suitcase felt absurdly light. I began to breathe great gusts of air, but there was little air to breathe.

I walked across Bull Ring and up Moorgate. Suddenly I began to feel excited and buoyant, and I was almost running by the time I reached Town Square. I began to whistle 'March of the Movies' and to march in step with it. There was nobody about. When I came to the War Memorial I transferred my suitcase to my right hand and at the correct moment I saluted with the left – up, two, three, down, two, three, head erect, shoulders back. I brought the whistling to a huffing crescendo and wheeled smartly into Infirmary Street. I dropped into a normal step, and then I began the slow walk home.

Suggestions for Coursework

Here are some questions designed to help you acquire detailed knowledge and understanding of *Billy Liar*. They are for you to discuss, make notes on, write about, and dramatise. Your teacher will specify whether you should work on your own, in pairs, or groups, and whether your conclusions should be presented verbally or in writing.

These questions fall into two sections:

The first asks you detailed questions about each chapter, and you can consider them as you go along, or return to them after reading the whole story.

The second asks you to look at Billy and the other characters in comparison with or in relation to other characters and events, thoughts, feelings, hopes, and experiences in other prose, poetry, and drama by different writers.

Both sections will help you to recognise and appreciate the ways in which Keith Waterhouse uses language, structure, and characterisation to achieve his effects, and will therefore enable you to produce work for both English Language and English Literature GCSE.

Looking back at the text

Chapter One

1 Billy is fed-up with his family. He writes, 'I began to plan entirely new parents for myself'.
What do we learn about Billy and his family in this chapter, and how realistic a picture of family life is it?
Some points to consider:
- What are the small, niggling ways in which each member of the family manages to irritate him?

- How does *he* irritate *them*?
- What sort of person would they like him to be and why is this so impossible? (Is this a common complaint in families with teenagers?)
- What do you think of his 'number 1' family?

2 Make a list of all the plans that Billy tells us about, in the order of their importance as you see them. Start with the least important (sucking a Polo mint right through?!) and move on from there. What do these plans tell you about him?

3 It's fairly clear already that Billy has a lot of problems: What are the main ones? Do you have any solutions? Make a chart like this:

PROBLEMS	SOLUTIONS
1 How to get rid of the calendars.	1 Put them in twenty different dustbins all round Stradhoughton.

Chapter Two

Billy observes people and places very acutely. In this chapter, we learn some things about Stradhoughton, Shadrack & Duxbury's where he works, and the people he works with. We not only learn some facts, however, but through his special observations we learn some more about *him*.

4 a) What do you think most people in Stradhoughton like about the place?
b) What does Billy *dis*like about it and poke fun at?
c) How do you think Shadrack sees himself and his life?
d) How does Billy see him?
e) How do you think Stamp sees himself?
f) How does Billy see him?
g) In what ways do you think Billy stands out as being different from the people around him?

5 Billy sometimes uses *satire* when he describes people and places.
(*Satire* is a way of speaking or writing which shows up the stupidities or faults of people's behaviour in a way which makes us laugh and criticise at the same time.) You can see

an example of his satire in his imagined conversation with Man o' the Dales on page 15. It is not the kind of conversation Billy could have with a straight face if they were really talking to each other, but maybe it *is* almost the kind of conversation that Man o' the Dales would enjoy. Billy has taken an almost accurate example of the way he talks and has pushed it just a bit further to satirise it. Billy invites you to laugh at him and to see him for what he really is – a bit pompous, self-deluding, parochial.[1]
Find an example of satire in Chapter One.

6 Now try writing these:
   a) Write a realistic description of your own area.
   b) Now rewrite your description using the style Man o' the Dales would use. (Remember, when he describes Stradhoughton, he pretends it is 'olde-worlde'; he sees 'gleaming cobbled streets' where there is only an ordinary high street.)

Chapter Three

7 Arthur says to Billy, 'The trouble with you, Cocker, is you're a pathological bloody liar.' He means Billy can't help lying as his lies are like a disease. (Pathology is the study of disease.) Give some examples of Billy's lies and show how one lie leads to another.

8 Show how the Kit-Kat Café is one of the features of Stradhoughton which Billy finds especially easy to satirise.
(To help you, look back at the definition of satire at the beginning of question 5. What is Stradhoughton trying to be? What is it really like?)

9 Billy says, 'Everybody I knew spoke in clichés, but Rita spoke as though she got her words out of a slot machine'.
   a) What else does he say about her?
   b) If he thinks there's so much wrong with her, why does he go on seeing her?

10 Arthur tells him, 'You're going to be up for bloody bigamy, mate, that's what you're going to be up for'.
What do you think is going to happen to Billy, Rita, and Barbara?

[1] a narrow outlook; he only knows about his own little world. ('Parochial' literally means 'of the parish'.)

Write a scene, as in a play or a chapter, in which all three meet unexpectedly.

11 Imagine a scene in which Rita is on the phone to a friend describing Billy and how they're getting on together.
Would her view of their relationship be roughly the same as his, or would we overhear a completely different one? Write out their conversation in play form.

Chapter Four

12 a) What does Billy like about Barbara?
b) What does he dislike about her?
c) What does he want from her?
Now ask those questions in reverse.
d) At the end of the chapter, Billy feels restless. Describe some of the thoughts *Barbara* might be having as she walks off down Market Street.

13 Billy and Barbara are acting out stereotypically male/female roles in this chapter.
Find evidence to support this statement and consider to what extent it helps them to be, or stops them from being, happy together.
Think about their lives at the moment and the future(s) they are both planning.

Chapter Five

14 There is a lot of tension in this chapter. Billy has a 'town branch' of his guilt chest which reminds him of all his unresolved worries. Then, in his interview with Shadrack, he has to struggle with his conscience, his sense of humour (which he has to try to suppress), and his growing rage.
Compile a list of these tensions, and then decide whether or not you feel some sympathy for him.

15 With a partner, act out the embarrassing scene in which Shadrack overhears Billy calling his name. This time add a different ending in which Shadrack makes it clear that he *has* heard.

Chapter Six

16 Billy arrives home after his difficult interview with Shadrack

and finds himself in the middle of a family row. What would it be like if he were coming home to his *imaginary* family? Write this chapter using his 'number 1' mother, father and grandmother. Use the last lines of Chapter Five (page 58) to help you.

17 Billy's father says, 'Don't melodram me with your fancy talk!' Billy says he was 'seized not with fear or anger but with sheer helplessness at the thought that these were beautiful Josiah Olroyd lines', and he 'could not even point them out to anybody, or even scoff'.
Have you been noticing how Billy observes people's speech patterns, funny words and phrases, and stock verbal responses to things?
It enables him to mock someone like Man o' the Dales, and he and Arthur can successfully mimic the people at work.
This is the author using language very cleverly to give you a clearer picture of the characters and of Billy's observation of them – and therefore an even clearer picture of *him*.
See if you can find some examples.

18 Billy keeps on feeling alternately excited and apprehensive about going to London. How realistic *is* this dream?

19 a) Why is Billy so unexpectedly moved by his encounter with Councillor Duxbury?
b) What did you think about it?
c) In realising that he could have confided in Councillor Duxbury, Billy misses a chance to really talk and share – and he realises that he has. This ties in with something else that Waterhouse writes about Billy: 'He had no friends, only allies.'
Can you imagine Billy as a genuine friend?

Chapter Seven

20 In trying to untangle all the lies he has told Barbara, Billy can't help telling a few more as well.
For which of them here do you feel the most sympathy: Billy or Barbara?

21 There is generally a difference between Billy's inner thoughts and what he actually says. Show how this is true in this chapter.

22 Billy wants some sort of sexual contact with Barbara. He also wants a degree of understanding, a kind of intimate

companionship which never seems to happen. What goes wrong? Look for some answers by exploring aspects such as the settings he chooses, the language of their talks, and the attitudes they strike.

Chapter Eight

23 For Billy, Liz is different from the other girls.
He even thinks he could tell her honestly about the muddle he has got himself into with Rita and Barbara. What do you think she would say? Imagine this conversation: Would Liz be cross with him? Would she feel put off and walk away? Would she be amused? Would she be calm and give him some advice?
Write what might take place as if it were the next chapter.

24 What is the effect of beginning this chapter with the scene with Rita and then moving on to Liz?

Chapter Nine

25 When Billy finishes his act, he gets down off the stage very quickly, with deep embarrassment.
   a) Note down all the reasons for this embarrassment.
   b) In what ways does this chapter show that Billy might be a part of, as well as estranged from, the society that makes up Stradhoughton?

26 Write down the thoughts that might have been running through Billy's father's head as he watched Billy on stage.

Chapter Ten

27 In groups of four, read aloud the passage where Billy meets Barbara and Rita who are confronting each other. (You'll need Billy, Barbara, Rita and a narrator.)

28 When Billy strides rapidly away from them, what do you think happens next between the two girls?
Write out this scene in play form.

29 Reread the paragraph beginning, 'My palms gritty with sweat . . .', and illustrate with photographs or drawings the scene it describes.

Chapter Eleven

30 Billy learns more about Liz this time. In what ways are they alike? In what ways does she make him feel happier and safer and most at ease with himself?

31 Although Billy feels good with Liz, he still keeps talking to her on a jokey level, as if he is afraid to let the relationship get more serious. He wants to be honest and he also still likes trying on expressions and using different voices. Find and note down these different sides of Billy.

32 If you were a friend of his at this point, what advice would you give him?

Chapter Twelve

33 We know how Billy feels when he arrives home: straightaway he gets shouted at; he feels trapped. He wants to go upstairs to get away, to check his guilt chest, to shut out the sound of his dad's voice. He wants to sit quietly and mull over what has happened with Liz, and what his future might hold.
What does his *father* feel?
Write this chapter from his father's point of view. (Remember, he's worried about the grandmother. As he sees it, Billy does not care about anybody but himself. He feels angry, hopeless, disgusted and anxious. Remember too that he has been ringing Billy without success all evening.)

Chapter Thirteen

34 Even while Billy's mother is telling him about his grandmother, Billy is restless. When he is told of her death, he says, 'please God, let me *feel* something'.
What is it that he finds so difficult about being at the hospital?
Did you expect him to react like this? Do you have any sympathy for him?

35 Reread the end of this chapter from 'Your grandma has died . . .' and then rewrite it as if his mother is telling this part of the story.

36 Billy's restlessness, sense of humour, sense of *separateness* from his family are almost hardening him at this point. Is this a contradiction in terms of his character – is the author going

too far in your opinion? Or are these tensions part of what *makes* him Billy?

Chapter Fourteen

37 Did you think Billy would go to London?
Draw up two columns: in one, write all the reasons why he might have gone, and in the other, give the reasons for his staying.
Sum up the likelihood of this dream becoming a reality.

38 Throughout the story, Billy has retreated into Ambrosia. What does this dream world provide him with that the real world does not?

39 Reality intrudes when Billy meets Rita in this chapter. Why is she so angry? What does she say that is so sharp and hurtful? Do you feel you understand why she's like this? What effect does she have on him?

40 Write an alternative ending for *Billy Liar.*

Looking at other writers

The female perspective

Rita, Barbara and Liz

Billy is excited, irritated, trapped, moved, angry, restless – and a whole lot else. He cracks jokes, has dreams, lies, deceives, is ambitious – we know a lot about him! What do we know about the young women who seem to have to dance around him?

We know some of the things they each feel about *him*; we know very little about what hidden feelings they may have, or what kinds of hopes and dreams they may have for their own life apart from some of the cosy images thrown up in those brief encounters. What do you think happens to them inside when they realise that Billy does not or can not give the things he seems to promise?

Here are some poems by Sharon Bell: they give us the female perspective.

Here are some poems by Sharon Bell: they give us the female perspective.

Walk Away

I thought . . .
It doesn't
matter
now.
I suppose, I
suppose I thought . . .
I remember
waiting.
Long hours of
no sleep
and times
of complete
oblivion
to the
rest of
the world.
Anxious
and
stagnant.
Waiting.
I thought . . .
I stopped thinking!
I knew!
I was *ANGRY*
and
you
were definitely
to blame.

Joanne

The women blame the
women so the men
don't get no blame
So many things changing
while so many stay
the same.

The Man

The man
don't belong to
NO ONE and
as the two
women in his life
it's something we
got to understand.
He don't have
two to belong
to one
He done got two
so he can do
what HE
wants to do –
either to me or he
can do it to you.

Remember Me?

Remember me
I am the one you will
never forget
Remember me
I am the women who
was more independant
than you, more outgoing
than you and more
outspoken than you.
Remember me
I am the one who
loved than left
(the one who you said would
always love and leave)
Remember me
I am forever remembering you.

1 Write some poems that Liz might have written to express her thoughts about her own life and her feelings for and about Billy.
2 Find some poems written by at least three other women

and/or one short story or novel written by a woman. Write an essay comparing those writers' views and treatment of women with the way Keith Waterhouse writes about Rita, Barbara, and Liz.

Mothers

We do not get to know Billy's mother very well. We see her through Billy's eyes and we really know only about the practical tasks she performs to keep the home going, how down-to-earth she is and therefore how much she irritates him. The only human, personal and revealing moment is when she is at the hospital when Gran dies. (And Billy shrugs off her grief then, too.)

Here's a poem which gives us a vision of the warmth someone feels for her mother. Two others which follow give the woman's own view; firstly of the joy she experiences in her new baby and then, quite differently, of the fierce sense of herself as a woman as well as a mother.

Praise Song for My Mother

You were
water to me
deep and bold and fathoming

You were
moon's eye to me
pull and grained and mantling

You were
sunrise to me
rise and warm and streaming

You were
the fishes red gill to me
the flame tree's spread to me
the crab's leg/the fried plantain smell
                                        replenishing replenishing

Go to your wide futures, you said

Grace Nichols

The Miracle

Before you were conceived
I wanted you
Before you were born
I loved you
Before you were here an hour
I would die for you
This is the miracle of life.
The pain, so great,
was more than the throbbing of your final journey
into my love
But part of a process
that came accompanied with
New Life
New Consciousness
New Understanding
New Wisdom
A bigger heart
To accommodate
New Love
At last Liberation
At last Freedom
How special, how valuable
How close to all things right
Nine months of worry and expectation
Brought more than imagination can conjure
Never really knew
Until . . .
I feel you coming
I am ready for you
I am ready for life
I am rejuvenated
I am Blessed
with the gift of life.

Maureen Hawkins

Don't Call Me Mama

Don't call me Mama
Don't call me Mother
See me for what I am
A Woman.

Even though you crawled
I pushed you out from under me.
I teased you with my breast.
It gave me pain
It gave me pleasure
It gave you life.

Don't call me Mama
A stalwart of the nation.
Don't call me Mother
The backbone of the struggle.
See me here for what I am
A Woman.

Throughout our history
You call me Mother.
You ban your belly
And call me Mama.
How much longer?
Will you learn?
My Motherhood is not my Womanhood
Just another dimension
of me
A Woman.

I am here in the struggle
I am here – part of the nation
I am here in Afrika
I am here in Britain
I am here in the Caribbean
I am here in the Americas
I am here on the Frontline
A Woman.

Mama, Mother
A sign of respect.
When you call me Mama
Do you see my Woman?
When you struggle for sustenance
between my breasts,
Call me Mother, Tower of Strength,
Keeper of Tradition
Do you see my Woman?

Before my belly bloated with another life,
My teeth clenched
and the sweat of labour
burnt my eyes
I was Woman.
Before you called me
Before you whispered 'Mother'
Before you cried out 'Mama'
I was Woman.

When you mourn my passing
Mourn my Woman.
Don't call me Mama
Don't call me Mother
See me for what I am
A Woman.

Carole Stewart

1 Write a letter from a daughter to a mother. The daughter is around your age, and has come to know some new things about her mother and to see her and value her in a new light.
2 Read Chapter Thirteen again. Rewrite it, not as if you are Billy's mother, but as if you are the author describing what happens there with a new sympathy for her. Billy says, 'for the first time she would be looking as though things had really happened'. If you were choosing to present her as a deeper, more sensitive character, better able to detect and articulate her own feelings, what would you want to write in Chapter Thirteen?

I'll love you forever

Billy has three different girl-friends and he says he loves them all.

Can you love more than one person? What does he mean? He uses the word 'love' very easily: is this because he's using it lightly, or because he doesn't understand what he's saying, or he really feels he *does* love all three?

Whatever *he* feels, there is deep frustration and unhappiness for *them*.

This is Sir John Suckling, writing in the seventeenth century:

The Constant Lover

Out upon it, I have loved
  Three whole days together!
And am like to love three more,
  If it hold fair weather.

Time shall moult away his wings
  Ere he shall discover
In the whole wide world again
  Such a constant lover.

But a pox upon't, no praise
  There is due at all to me:
Love with me had made no stay,
  Had it any been but she.

Had it any been but she,
  And that very very face,
There had been at least ere this
  A dozen dozen in her place.

Of course, girls can do this too!

Here is a poem by W H Auden, a twentieth-century poet:

As I Walked out One Evening

As I walked out one evening,
  Walking down Bristol Street,
The crowds upon the pavement
  Were fields of harvest wheat.

And down by the brimming river
  I heard a lover sing
Under an arch of the railway
  'Love has no ending.

'I'll love you, dear, I'll love you
  Till China and Africa meet,
And the river jumps over the mountain
  And the salmon sing in the street,

'I'll love you till the ocean
  Is folded and hung up to dry
And the seven stars go squawking
  Like geese about the sky.

The years shall run like rabbits,
  For in my arms I hold
The Flower of the Ages,
  And the first love of the world.'

But all the clocks in the city
  Began to whirr and chime:
'O let not Time deceive you,
  You cannot conquer Time.

'In the burrows of the Nightmare
  Where Justice naked is,
Time watches from the shadow
  And coughs when you would kiss.

'In headaches and in worry
  Vaguely life leaks away,
And Time will have his fancy
  To-morrow or to-day.

'Into many a green valley
  Drifts the appalling snow;
Time breaks the threaded dances
  And the diver's brilliant bow.

'O plunge your hands in water,
  Plunge them in up to the wrist;
Stare, stare in the basin
  And wonder what you've missed.

'The glacier knocks in the cupboard,
  The desert sighs in the bed,
And the crack in the tea-cup opens
  A lane to the land of the dead.

'Where the beggars raffle the banknotes
  And the Giant is enchanting to Jack,
And the Lily-white Boy is a Roarer,
  And Jill goes down on her back.

'O look, look in the mirror,
  O look in your distress;
Life remains a blessing
  Although you cannot bless.

'O stand, stand at the window
  As the tears scald and start;
You shall love your crooked neighbour
  With your crooked heart.'

It was late, late in the evening,
  The lovers they were gone;
The clocks had ceased their chiming,
  And the deep river ran on.

1 Write a comic four-verse poem, as if written by Billy, in which he dedicates a verse each to Barbara, Rita and Liz. What will you put in the fourth verse?
2 Write a comic-strip story in which a boy or girl loses a boy-friend or girl-friend when someone else comes along. What ending will you give it?
When you have finished that, write about the same characters and events *as a short story*. This time, you will have to 'flesh out' the story, give a deeper version.

Proposals

Billy's talks about marriage have an air of unreality about them. When Barbara says, 'Let's talk about our cottage, pet', *we* know he's just playing for time while the 'passion pills' work. Part of him likes the idea of being married; another – very big! – part does not.

H G Wells describes a proposal in his book *The History of Mr Polly*: like Billy, Mr Polly finds himself in the middle of a difficult situation, and one he may not be able to get himself out of!

He put an arm over the back of the seat, and assumed a more comfortable attitude. He glanced at Miriam, who was sitting in a lax, thoughtful pose, with her eyes on the flowers. She was wearing her old dress. She had not had time to change, and the blue tones of her old dress brought out a certain warmth in her skin, and her pose exaggerated whatever was feminine in her rather lean and insufficient body, and rounded her flat chest delusively. A little line of light lay across her profile. The afternoon was full of transfiguring sunshine, children were playing noisily in the adjacent sand-pit, some Judas trees were abloom in the villa gardens that bordered the recreation ground, and all the place was bright with touches of young summer colour. It all merged with the effect of Miriam in Mr Polly's mind.

Her thought found speech. 'One did ought to be happy in a shop,' she said, with a note of unusual softness in her voice.

It seemed to him that she was right. One did ought to be happy in a shop. Folly not to banish dreams that made one ache of townless woods and bracken tangles and red-haired linen-clad figures sitting in dappled sunshine upon grey and crumbling walls and looking queenly down on one with clear blue eyes. Cruel and foolish dreams they were, that ended in one's being laughed at and made a mock of. There was no mockery here.

'A shop's such a respectable thing to be,' said Miriam thoughtfully.

'*I* could be happy in a shop,' he said.

His sense of effect had made him pause.

'If I had the right company,' he added.

She became very still.

Mr Polly swerved a little from the conversational ice-run upon which he had embarked.

'I'm not such a blooming Geezer,' he said, 'as not to be able to sell goods a bit. One has to be nosy over one's buying, of course. But I shall do all right.'

He stopped, and felt falling, falling through the aching silence that followed.

'If you get the right company,' said Miriam.

'I shall get that all right.'

'You don't mean you've got some one —— ?'

He found himself plunging.

'I've got someone in my eye this minute,' he said.

'Elfrid,' she said, turning to him. 'You don't mean —— '

Well, *did* he mean? 'I do!' he said.

'Not reely!' She clenched her hands to keep still.

He took the conclusive step.

'Well, you and me, Miriam, in a little shop, with a cat and a canary —— ' He tried too late to get back to a hypothetical note. 'Just suppose it!'

'You mean,' said Miriam, 'you're in love with me, Elfrid?'

What possible answer can a man give to such a question but 'Yes!'

Regardless of the public park, the children in the sand-pit, and everyone, she bent forward and seized his shoulder and kissed him on the lips. Something lit up in Mr Polly at the touch. He put an arm about her and kissed her back, and felt an irrevocable act was sealed. He had a curious feeling that it would be very satisfying to marry and have a wife – only somehow he wished it wasn't Miriam. Her lips were very pleasant to him, and the feel of her in his arm.

They recoiled a little from each other, and sat for a moment flushed and awkwardly silent. His mind was altogether incapable of controlling its confusions.

'I didn't dream,' said Miriam, 'you cared —— Sometimes I thought it was Annie, sometimes Minnie —— '

'Always I liked you better than them,' said Mr Polly.

'I love you, Elfrid,' said Miriam, 'since ever we met at your poor father's funeral. Leastways I *would* have done if I had thought ——You didn't seem to mean anything you said.

'I can't believe it!' she added.

'Nor I,' said Mr Polly.

'You mean to marry me and start that little shop?'

'Soon as ever I find it,' said Mr Polly.

'I had no more idea when I came out with you —— '

'Nor me.'

'It's like a dream.'

They said no more for a little while.

'I got to pinch myself to think it's real,' said Miriam.

'What they'll do without me at 'ome I can't imagine.

When I tell them —— ''

For the life of him Mr Polly could not tell whether he was full of tender anticipations or regretful panic.

'Mother's no good at managing – not a bit. Annie don't care for housework, and Minnie's got no 'ead for it. What they'll do without me I can't imagine.'

'They'll have to do without you,' said Mr Polly, sticking to his guns.

A clock in the town began striking.

'Lor!' said Miriam, 'we shall miss Annie, sitting 'ere and love-making.'

She rose and made as if to take Mr Polly's arm. But Mr Polly felt that their condition must be nakedly exposed to the ridicule of the world by such a linking, and evaded her movement.

Annie was already in sight before a flood of hesitation and terrors assailed Mr Polly.

Don't tell anyone yet a bit,' he said.

'Only Mother,' said Miriam firmly.

1 Do you think Miriam and Mr Polly will be happy together? Do you think Billy will get as far as actually making a proposal he will stick to?
Write a story about a relationship in which one partner is destined to be very unhappy. What makes she or he think there *will* be happiness? What are the warning signs? What happens, and how does it end?
2 Find the passage in Chapter Fourteen where Billy and Liz meet at the station, and she says, 'I'm not coming, you know, Billy.'

She wants to marry him, not to share the 'communal ring', but to live a more adult, loving and committed life. Importantly she does not think it means giving up adventures; she would like to share them with him.
Rewrite the chapter to give Billy a way of saying he would like this too.
You could write another chapter showing how this version of the story turns out.

Saying goodbye

Billy doesn't seem to know how to say goodbye and so his muddles with his different girl-friends just go on. Remember how he finally (?) says goodbye to Liz near the end of the book?

Liz says she will go to London with him – on one condition . . . .

> I closed my eyes tightly and smote my forehead, teetering on the brink of a decision. All the details of it were there, in a compact parcel of No. 1 thinking, from the register office ceremony to the Chelsea attic. All it needed was the decision.
>
> 'And *I* wouldn't want the communal ring,' said Liz. But *I* did not answer, and she knew that there was no answer.
>
> A porter was rattling the gate at the entrance to the Doncaster platform. Liz picked up her bag, a small, well-worn grip. She regarded me steadily for a few seconds and, standing a foot in front of me, blew me a kiss.
>
> 'Postcards?' she said, whispering it.
>
> 'Postcards,' I said.
>
> I struck the farewell attitude, legs apart, arms akimbo, the sad figure fading into silhouette as the train steams away. But she did not look back. The porter banged the gate shut and I saw Liz clamber into the last carriage after two soldiers. I watched the train disappear.

Here are two quite different poems in which someone says goodbye.

Goodbye

So we must say Goodbye, my darling,
And go, as lovers go, for ever;
Tonight remains, to pack and fix on labels
And make an end of lying down together.

I put a final shilling in the gas,
And watch you slip your dress below your knees
And lie so still I hear your rustling comb
Modulate the autumn in the trees.

And all the countless things I shall remember
Lay mummy-cloths of silence round my head;
I fill the carafe with a drink of water;
You say, 'We paid a guinea for this bed,'

And then, 'We'll leave some gas, a little warmth
For the next resident, and these dry flowers,'
And turn your face away, afraid to speak
The big word, that Eternity is ours.

Your kisses close my eyes and yet you stare
As though God struck a child with nameless fears;
Perhaps the water glitters and discloses
Time's chalice and its limpid useless tears.

Everything we renounce except ourselves;
Selfishness is the last of all to go;
Our sighs are exhalations of the earth,
Our footprints leave a track across the snow.

We made the universe to be our home,
Our nostrils took the wind to be our breath,
Our hearts are massive towers of delight,
We stride across the seven seas of death.

Yet when all's done you'll keep the emerald
I placed upon your finger in the street;
And I will keep the patches that you sewed
On my old battledress tonight, my sweet.

Alun Lewis

25.40 p.m. (past mourning)

twenty five
and she waited
and him sooon come
and she waited

she waited
till he bought a draw
till he checked a spar
till he did some runnings
till he looked up an ex-girl friend
and she waited
and him sooon come
and she waited

she waited
till he got his shit together
till he found himself
till he got a job
till he made it
and she waited
and him sooon come
and she waited

she waited
in her party clothes
outside supermarkets with shopping bags full
lying in that big empty bed
groaning in hospital holding her fat belly
and she waited
and him sooon come
andshewaited

she waited
for dreams to come true
for the phone to ring
for the door to knock
for a sign

and she waited
and him sooon come
and she waited

she waited
in darkened rooms
hating her reflection
eating herself silly
drinking herself blind
AND SHE WAITED
and him sooon come
and

                                        she waited

Until one day
she looked at her watch
fifteen years had gone by
could it be   she was running fast?
(or maybe *he* was running slow)
Either way she had waited long enough
The Waiting Game was no more fun
She picked up herself
                    and walked out the door
She was forty
          and her life had just begun

a-dZiko Simba

In this extract from *Summer of My German Soldier* by Bette Greene, a young girl called Patty has to say goodbye to Anton whom she has helped to hide, who is much older, and who now must leave . . . .

I left my sack at the foot of the garage steps and crawled my way up through the blackness. 'Anton,' I whispered. But behind the closed door, there was only silence. A feeling of loss swept over me. 'Anton!' I cried, hitting the door with my fist. 'It's me, Patty!'

Abruptly the door opened. 'Quiet!' As he led me through the blackness I tried to find my voice. 'I thought, I thought you had gone,' I said and then from somewhere came crying. Only after my tongue had tasted saltiness did I know its source.

Anton squeezed my hand.

'I'm sorry,' I said. 'I didn't know I was going to do that.'

Anton brought my hand to the slightly moist inner corners of his own eyes. 'Just wanted to point out that the biggest difference between us is that you cry more noisily than I.'

I laughed, feeling grateful for the darkness which concealed my eyes.

'We both knew that I couldn't stay. It had to happen. P.B. you always knew that.'

'No, I didn't!' I breathed in deep. 'Anton – ' I needed to say his name aloud again as though it were a magical incantation 'Anton, I won't even be that much trouble. What I'm trying to tell you is – ' The hurdle felt too high for vaulting.

'P.B., I don't think –'

'Don't talk. Listen to me.' It was my hurdle, and I had to clear it myself. 'I don't think you oughta leave me, not now. I haven't learned all those things you were going to teach me – things about Emerson [1] and – and – Oh, Anton, let me be with you, go where you go.'

His thumb pressed against my palm. 'You know what you are asking is impossible, but if you're saying that you love me –'

'Yes,' I answered, wondering if it came out audibly. 'Yes.'

'Then know this, Patty, it's not completely one-sided. I love you too, and in my own way I'll miss you.'

He opened the door, climbed quickly down, and offered up his hand to me.

Outside, the moon, almost full-grown now, threw soft illumination on his forehead and cheeks while leaving the deeper recesses in shadows. Then it struck me that if someday I grow old and forgetful, forgetting even friends' names and faces, his face I could never forget.

He looked down at the luminous hands of his watch. 'The train comes by about ten fifteen.'

'Yes,' I replied and then, thinking that my answer sounded curt, I added, 'Yes, it does.'

'Let me help you back into the house,' he offered. 'There's still time.'

[1] A famous American thinker and writer.

I began to feel jealous of time and trivia. Of last moments consumed in pass-the-salt type of comments. 'No thanks. My bedroom window screen is unhooked and the water spigot is there, makes a good foothold.'

'Well, I must say good-bye now.'

'Oh, I almost forgot,' I dug into the right-hand pocket of my jeans. 'Here's some money – only four dollars and sixty-five cents. It's all Ruth and I had.'

He took the money. 'Thanks for this, for everything. And I have something for you too. It belonged to my father and his father and even his father before that.' Anton looked down at his hand. Then warm metal encircled my finger. 'This ring was made by Germany's most famous goldsmith for my great-grandfather when he was president of the university of Gottingen. The crest represents the office of the president.'

A thing of value! He'd give it to me? 'Maybe you'd better keep it, Anton. I mean, it has been in your family for so long.' My tongue! I could bite it off. The ring had been mine for only a moment, and now I would lose that too.

'The greater the value, the greater the pleasure in giving it. The ring is yours, P.B.' Then in the darkened silence, I heard him breathe in deeply. 'Am I still your teacher?' Without pausing for an answer he continued, 'Then I want you to learn this, our last, lesson. Even if you forget everything else I want you to always remember that you are a person of value, and you have a friend who loved you enough to give you his most valued possession.'

'I will, Anton. I'll remember.'

I saw or felt it coming – my chin tilted up as my eyes closed. Then our lips touched, lingered together briefly before going their own separate ways. When I opened my eyes Anton was gone.

Time passed. I stood rigid and unmoving, wanting nothing new to happen to me. New time was nothing except a way to determine how long he had been gone. From under the weight of my foot I felt a chinaberry being pushed into the damp ground. My finger passed over the indented crest of the gold ring.

Then from down the distant tracks came the ten fifteen.

1 Take these three 'goodbyes' and show in what ways they are similar and different. What feelings do they express? How does each gain from the form of text used, i.e. rhyming verse, free verse, prose? What moves you most and why? Do they remind you of anything else you have read (or experienced)?
2 Take one or other of the poems and tell the story behind it.

Families

Billy's attempts to escape from his family, by inventing a new one and by trying to leave for London, do not get him very far.

Their Plan

Who says
  I should wear a skirt

Who says
  The Earth is dirt

Who says
  I should look like you

Who says
  I should do as you do

Who says
  It's time to eat

Who says
  I should eat meat

Who says
  I should comb my hair

Who says
  The best is 'fair'

I am
  What I am
I'll do what
  I can
to destroy
  Their plan

Sista Roots

In *Brave New World*, published in 1932, Aldous Huxley sets a story way in the future (the seventh century AF – After Ford) where babies are born from test-tubes (no longer Science Fiction!) and families do not exist. Here, some students are told what it used to be like.

'Once upon a time,' the Director began, 'while our Ford was still on earth, there was a little boy called Reuben Rabinovitch. Reuben was the child of Polish-speaking parents.' The Director interrupted himself. 'You know what Polish is, I suppose?'

'A dead language.'

'Like French and German,' added another student, officiously showing off his learning.

'And "parent"?' questioned the D.H.C.

There was an uneasy silence. Several of the boys blushed. They had not yet learned to draw the significant but often very fine distinction between smut and pure science. One, at last, had the courage to raise a hand.

'Human beings used to be . . .' he hesitated; the blood rushed to his cheeks. 'Well, they used to be viviparous.'

'Quite right.' The Director nodded approvingly.

'And when the babies were decanted . . .'

'"Born",' came the correction.

'Well, then they were the parents – I mean, not the babies, of course; the other ones.' The poor boy was overwhelmed with confusion.

'In brief,' the Director summed up, 'the parents were the father and the mother.' The smut that was really science fell with a crash into the boys' eye-avoiding silence. 'Mother,' he repeated loudly, rubbing in the science; and, leaning back in his chair, 'These,' he said gravely, 'are unpleasant facts; I know it. But, then, most historical facts *are* unpleasant.'

He returned to Little Reuben – to Little Reuben, in whose room, one evening by an oversight, his father and mother (crash, crash!) happened to leave the radio turned on.

('For you must remember that in those days of gross viviparous reproduction, children were always brought up by their parents and not in the State Conditioning Centres.') . . .

Mustapha Mond leaned forward, shook a finger at them: 'Just try to realise it,' he said, and his voice sent a strange thrill quivering along their diaphragms. 'Try to realise what it was like to have a viviparous mother.'

That smutty word again. But none of them dreamed, this time, of smiling.

'Try to imagine what "living with one's family" meant.'

'And do you know what a "home" was?'

They shook their heads . . .

'And home was as squalid psychically as physically. Psychically, it was a rabbit hole, a midden, hot with the frictions of tightly packed life, reeking with emotion. What suffocating intimacies, what dangerous, insane, obscene relationships between the members of the family group! Maniacally, the mother brooded over her children (*her* children) . . . brooded over them like a cat over its kittens; but a cat that could talk, a cat that could say, "My baby, my baby" over and over again. "My baby, and oh, oh, at my breast, the little hands, the hunger, and that unspeakable agonising pleasure! Till at last my baby sleeps with a bubble of white milk at the corner of his mouth. My little baby sleeps . . ."

'Yes,' said Mustapha Mond, nodding his head, 'you may well shudder.' . . .

Mother, monogamy, romance. High spurts the fountain; fierce and foamy the wild jet. The urge has but a single outlet. My love, my baby. No wonder those poor pre-moderns were mad and wicked and miserable. Their world didn't allow them to take things easily, didn't allow them to be sane, virtuous, happy. What with mothers and lovers, what with the prohibitions they were not conditioned to obey, what with the temptations and the lonely remorses, what with all the diseases and the endless isolating pain, what with the uncertainties and the poverty – they were forced to feel strongly. And feeling strongly (and strongly, what was more, in solitude, in hopelessly individual isolation), how could they be stable? . . .

1 Although Billy spends a lot of time thinking about how to leave his family, Keith Waterhouse chooses to end the book with '. . . and then I began the slow walk home'. It seems

as if Billy can not finally bring himself to break from them. Perhaps they support him as much as they irritate him .... Write an essay called: *A View of the Family as seen by Keith Waterhouse.*
If you have read anything else by him, and any other books by other writers which give a view of family life, this would widen your terms of reference. You could then call your essay: *A View of Family Life as seen in X number of different books.* You could sub-title it with the names of those books.

2 Write a final chapter, Chapter Fifteen, in which Billy wakes up the morning after his return home. What is he thinking and feeling now?

Grandparents

We only see Billy's Gran as an irritant. She is nosy, bossy and querulous. But some people get on well with their grand-parents. They love them and are even inspired by them. The poem below, called *Grandad*, was written by the author at the age of fourteen on a visit to South Africa. He visited his grandfather on Robben Island, which is a top-security island prison for political prisoners, and where in 1962 Nelson Mandela was imprisoned (at the time of writing he is still there). We get a very powerful sense of the grandfather's presence. On a second reading, you can see that the whole poem is building up to those last six lines.

Grandad

If someone were to ask me what
  it's like to visit Robben Island I
  would tell them to ask another
  question
If someone were to ask me what it's
  like to visit a relation who has
  already done twenty-one years
  in prison, and is looking at the same
  again

I would tell that person the visiting
room is a wide corridor split down
the middle with a thick, sound-proof
wall, there are fourteen cubicles and
you look through a tiny double
glazed window with a movable
steel plate in the middle
I would tell that person that the
way you talk is through a telephone
with a warder listening in
I would tell that person that they will
run out of things to say after three
minutes and it's embarrassing when
you've waited a year to see the person
If someone were to ask me what it
feels like to sit on a hard bench and talk for three hours
down a phone
I would tell that person that when
they leave they will want a wheelchair
as the whole experience is extremely
physically and mentally tiring
I would tell that person that after
having a telephone receiver pressed
hard against an ear for two hours
your arm turns to jelly and your
ear feels like it's got a hundred
pounds hanging from the lobe
And then, after telling that person what
it's like
I would tell that person that the only
thing you can feel coming off a
seventy-two year old who's nearly
spent a quarter of a century behind
bars is strength
Strength radiates from behind his thick glasses
Strength radiates from his arthritic hands
Strength radiates from his grey hair
Strength radiates from his jaw line
Strength radiates from his soul
Strength radiates

Manelisi

1 What other stories and poems have you come across that feature a much older person? Are these older people depicted as easy to get on with? Are they special people to love and admire? Or are they difficult like Billy's Gran?
Compare these other writings with *Billy Liar*: show how the authors present a certain view of older people in general or of one person in particular.
Say which you find the most sympathetic, or realistic, and why.
2 Write a story or poem about an older person you have known well and/or have lived closely with.

Having a dream

Billy dreams of leaving his home and family and going to London to be a famous writer. Here are three poems about having dreams: each writer is saying something quite deep and serious about how life and dreams go together.

The next poem is by Irina Ratushinskaya. She was sent to a Soviet hard-labour camp in April 1983. She suffered beatings, force-feeding and solitary confinement in brutal, freezing conditions, and became so gravely ill that many people feared she would not survive her sentence. Her crime was writing poetry. She was released in 1986 because people from all over the world protested that she should be set free. (You can read about her in a book called *No I'm Not Afraid.*)

In this poem she cheers herself up by dreaming that she possesses something that no-one in a prison could possibly have. You could say that her ability to have this dream is part of what helps her to keep having a more important dream: of a society which admires and cherishes all its writers.

Some people's dreams pay all their bills

Some people's dreams pay all their bills,
While others' gild an empty shell . . .
But mine go whimpering about a velvet dress,
Cherry-red and sumptuous as sin.
O, inaccessible! Not of our world!
Nowhere to get you, or to put you on . . .
But how I want you!
Against all reason's reproaches –
There, in the very narrows of the heart's
Recesses – flourishes the poison
Of heavy folds, and obscure embroidery . . .
The childish, flouted right
To beauty! Not bread, not domicile –
But unbleached, royal lace,
Enspiralled rings, sly ribbons – but no!
My day is like a donkey, bridled, laden,
My night deserted, like the prison light.
But in my soul – it's no good! I am guilty! –
I keep on sewing it, and in my mind I make
The thousandth stitch, as I do up my anorak
And try on my tarpaulin boots.

Langston Hughes was a celebrated Black American writer; and here he wonders what happens to the dream you put off trying to make come true . . .

Harlem

What happens to a dream deferred?

Does it dry up
like a raisin in the sun?
Or fester like a sore –
And then run?
Does it stink like rotten meat?
Or crust and sugar over –
like a syrupy sweet?

Maybe it just sags
like a heavy load.

Or does it explode?

Look at the photograph of Paul Potts, the next writer, before you go on to read his poem:

Note

My dreams
Watching me said
One to the other
This life has let us down

Paul Potts

1 Billy's family, trained to caution by years of pre-war austerity, can not begin to understand the dream of freedom that their son indulges in. They automatically respond with shouts of 'What about your job with Shadrack and Duxbury's?' and 'Who do you think is going to keep you?' It makes Billy see his life in terms of 'them and us'. In what ways do *you* see his capacity to dream as marking him out from the other characters in the book?

2 You can have dreams all of your own and dreams for everybody in your wider society. The Feminist movement in many countries has long had dreams of a life which gives girls and women equal opportunities. There have always been political writers, women and men, with dreams for the future. Their writing, whether for speeches, songs, in novels and poetry, in essays and much non-fiction, has the power to move and inspire. Sometimes writing is so powerful that books have been burnt. Think of some of these writers you may know about – many people, for example, may know about the speeches of Martin Luther King; ask other people for names which may readily come to mind. Look at what they have written and try to account for what it is that can be so powerful about their writing.

A sense of place

A 'sense of place' is something which features in many stories. It tells the reader about the setting. It also plays an important part in creating the atmosphere, and sometimes it contributes towards giving a more rounded, or deeper, picture of the characters in the story. Billy, for example, would probably be a different person, requiring a wholly different characterisation, if he came from a big city rather than a smallish northern industrial town. Look how Olive Senior, a Jamaican writer, describes her character Laura partly in terms of the landscape in her book *Summer Lightning*:

> She had grown up in a part of the mountain cockpits where a gravel road was the only thing that broke the monotony of the humpbacked hills and endless hills everywhere. There were so many hills that for half of the day their house and yard were damp and dark and moss grew on the sides of the clay path. It was only at midday when the sun was directly overhead that they received light. The houses were perched precariously up the hillsides with slippery paths leading to them from the road, and if anyone bothered to climb to the tops of the hills, all they would see was more mountains. Because it was so hilly the area seemed constantly to be in a dark blue haze, broken only by the occasional hibiscus or croton and the streams of brightly coloured birds dashing through the foliage. They were hemmed in by the mountains on all sides and Laura liked it, because all her life was spent in space that was enclosed and finite, protecting her from what dangers she did not even know.

1 Write about this 'sense of place', this powerful connection between people and where they come from. You could write about this experience in your own life, or you could describe and compare some of the books you have read in which the place has an important part to play.

2 This is what Billy is trying to escape from:

Stradhoughton's main street is . . .

> exactly like any other High Street in Great Britain. Woolworth's looked like Woolworth's, the Odeon looked like the Odeon, and the *Stradhoughton Echo's* own office . . . looked like a public lavatory in honest native white tile . . .

with . . .

> the bookies' shops, the stinking urinal, the sly chemist's with red rubber gloves and big sex books in the window, and the obscure one-man businesses mooning behind the dark doorways.

This is . . .

> the usual Saturday morning down in town, the fat women rolling along on their bad feet like toy clowns in pudding basins, the grey-faced men reviewing the sporting pinks.

. . . but this is not Stradhoughton as Keith Waterhouse is seeing it; this is Stradhoughton *as Billy sees it.*

One of the ways in which we know that Billy is clever, perceptive and *different* from the other characters in the book is this lethally sharp and mocking picture that he draws of the place he comes from. When Man o' the Dales conjures up 'sturdy buildings of honest native stone, gleaming cobbled streets', and other similar fancies, Billy wants to put him right on his facts. (So Billy uses 'honest native' to describe the lavatory-like white tiles.) 'The cobbled streets, gleaming or otherwise, had long ago been ripped up with the tram-lines . . .' When Shadrack replaces Duxbury's fake 'Dickensian windows, bottle-glass and all' with modern and equally ugly plate glass and stainless steel lettering, making a complete hash and confusion of the front of the shop, Billy notes that 'yet another piece of old Stradhoughton bit the dust and the new effect was of a chip shop on a suburban housing estate'. Find other examples of the way we a) build up a picture of Stradhoughton, and therefore b) come to know more about Billy.

Being a writer

Billy wants to be a professional writer. It is the strongest way in which he feels he will realise some of his dreams of fame and independence. This is an ambitious dream involving a lot of failures and very little money! When young people want to be professional writers, their parents often say, 'Get a steady job first and then see how you go!'

Wendy Cope in her poem below gives her opinion about how our society feels about its writers . . .

Engineers' Corner

Why isn't there an Engineers' Corner in Westminster Abbey? In Britain we've always made more fuss of a ballad than a blueprint . . . How many schoolchildren dream of becoming great engineers?

Advertisement placed in *The Times* by
the Engineering Council

We make more fuss of ballads than of blueprints –
That's why so many poets end up rich
While engineers scrape by in cheerless garrets.
Who needs a bridge or dam? Who needs a ditch?

Whereas the person who can write a sonnet
Has got it made. It's always been the way,
For everybody knows that we need poems
And everybody reads them every day.

Yes, life is hard if you choose engineering –
You're sure to need another job as well;
You'll have to plan your projects in the evenings
Instead of going out. It must be hell.

While well-heeled poets ride around in Daimlers,
You'll burn the midnight oil to earn a crust,
With no hope of a statue in the Abbey,
With no hope, even, of a modest bust.

No wonder small boys dream of writing couplets
And spurn the bike, the lorry and the train.
There's far too much encouragement for poets –
That's why this country's going down the drain.

But you are not only 'a writer' when you have been published; every time you write something, you are fulfilling that part of yourself which is just that – a writer. Writing for your GCSEs; keeping a diary; writing a letter; your personal story and poetry writing; any personal study writing . . . all this is properly called writing. Through your writing, you can make people laugh and brighten up their lives; you can explain yourself better, sometimes; you can move people; you can reach a wider audience than just one.

Langston Hughes reflects on how writing can have deep and lasting consequences in the poem that follows: it's about the misery of receiving a letter. It is a private kind of writing of which most people have some experience.

Little Old Letter

It was yesterday morning
I looked in my box for mail.
The letter that I found there
Made me turn right pale.

Just a little old letter,
Wasn't even one page long –
But it made we wish
I was in my grave and gone.

I turned it over,
Not a word writ on the back.
I never felt so lonesome
Since I was born black.

Just a pencil and paper,
You don't need no gun nor knife –
A little old letter
Can take a person's life.

1 Many of the Imprint books contain pieces by the writers which tell us something about why and how they came to write. Do some research of your own. Find out about the background of some writers of your choice – especially Keith Waterhouse, if you are studying *Billy Liar*. Write up your findings in a piece called:
Being a writer.
2 Write a story in which a letter plays a vital part.

Survival

Final Curve

When you turn the corner
And you run into *yourself*
Then you know that you have turned
All the corners that are left.

Langston Hughes

Still Here

I've been scarred and battered.
My hopes the wind done scattered.
Snow has friz me, sun has baked me.
    Looks like between 'em
    They done tried to make me
Stop laughin', stop lovin', stop livin –
    But I don't care!
    I'm still here!

Langston Hughes

The Last Laugh

I made hay while the sun shone.
  My work sold.
Now, if the harvest is over
  And the world cold,
Give me the bonus of laughter
  As I lose hold.

John Betjeman

Somehow, whatever happens to Billy, he manages to survive.

1 How many 'narrow misses' does he have? How is he affected at the time by each of these experiences? His mother says, 'If you're in trouble, Billy, it's not something you can leave behind you, you know . . . you put it in your suitcase and take it with you.' She says it in a shaky voice; she means well. But does he put his survival instinct down to luck? Intelligence? Good advice? Does he learn from anything? What

brings him home in the end? After studying these questions, write your thoughts down in notes and then in essay form under this title: *In what ways might Billy prove to be the same or a different person after everything that has happened to him?*

2 When Billy meets Councillor Duxbury in Chapter Six, he makes fun of him by speaking in the language he and Arthur have made up. It is a pretend northern dialect and the councillor is not deceived.

> He studied me keenly, and I realised for the first time, with a sinking heart, that he was not as daft as he looked.
> 'Is ta taking a rise out o' me, young man?'
> I felt myself flushing, and found my whole personality shifting into the familiar position of sheepishness and guilt. 'No, of course not.'
> 'Well just talk as thi mother and father brought thee up to talk then. Ah've had no education, ah had to educate myself, but that's no reason for thee to copy t' way *I* talk.' He spoke sharply but kindly, in a voice of authority with some kind of infinite wisdom behind it, and at that moment I felt genuinely ashamed.

His quiet authority and kindness makes Billy feel that here was a possible confidant if only he knew how to go about it. It shows up a big lack in his life – no real friend to share real and honest things with. It is why he values Liz – 'She was the only girl I knew who cared, or who could talk about things as if they really mattered. We began chattering, eagerly interrupting, laughing, grinning at each other as though we knew the whole joke about the world and understood it.' The limits to this relationship however are defined by how lasting her effect is – and it is not long: 'Sometimes I could think about Liz, think properly on the ordinary plane, for a full minute, before we were both whisked off into Ambrosia.'

To what extent does Billy scrape through to the end of the story on his own resources and to what extent is he helped along by anyone else? When you have decided, compare him with a character in *one* other book whom you feel has the same problem; of how to make real friends and draw on the best in them in order to lead a better or happier life.

Wider Reading

You will find a list of all the books Keith Waterhouse has written on pages 192–195. You might especially like to read *Billy Liar on the Moon, In the Mood*, and *Maggie Muggins*.

Here are some other books for students who would like to read more widely after studying *Billy Liar*.

Fiction

Some books by other writers of the same period in which *Billy Liar* was written (late '50s, carly '60s): you will find they provide some interesting contrasts and comparisons with Billy, his thoughts and experiences and preoccupations; with Stradhoughton; and with the times in which he lives.

BARSTOW, STAN, *The Human Element and other stories* (Longman Imprint Books)
BARSTOW, STAN, *A Kind of Loving* (Michael Joseph)
BARSTOW, STAN, *The Watchers on the Shore* (Corgi)
BRAINE, JOHN, *Room at the Top* (Penguin)
SILLITOE, ALAN, *The Loneliness of the Long Distance Runner* (Longman Imprint Books)
SILLITOE, ALAN, *Saturday Night and Sunday Morning* (Grafton)
STOREY, DAVID, *This Sporting Life* (Penguin)

Some books by women writing about love and loss, independence, growing up and all the other themes which you will have found in *Billy Liar*, this time seen with a woman's perception:

CARTER, ANGELA, *Heroes and Villains* (Penguin)
CARTER, ANGELA, *Wayward Girls and Wicked Women* (Virago)
PARK, CHRISTINE and HEATON, CAROLINE (EDS), *Close Company: Stories of Mothers and Daughters* (Virago)
WALKER, ALICE, *In Love and Trouble: Stories of Black Women* (The Women's Press)

WASHINGTON, MARY HELEN (ED), *Any Women's Blues: Stories by Contemporary Black Women Writers* (Virago)
WILLIAMS, JAY, *The Practical Princess and Other Liberating Fairy Tales* (Scholastic)
WINTERSON, JEANETTE (ED), *Passion Fruit: Romantic Fiction with a Twist* (Pandora)

Poetry

COSMAN, KEEFE and WEAVER (EDS), *The Penguin Book of Women Poets* (Penguin)
FOSTER, JOHN L, *Standpoints* (Nelson)
FOSTER, JOHN, *New Angles 1 & 2* (Oxford)
HEANEY, SEAMUS and HUGHES, TED (EDS), *The Rattle Bag* (Faber)
PATTEN, BRIAN, *Love Poems* (Unwin)
ROSEN, MICHAEL and JACKSON, DAVID (EDS), Speaking To You (Macmillan Education)
WALKER, ALICE, *Goodnight Willie Lee, I'll See You in the Morning* (The Women's Press)

Non-fiction

Listed below are some books which take up some of the gender issues raised in several of the questions in Section One and Two.

BERGER, JOHN, *Ways of Seeing* (BBC)
HEMMINGS, SUSAN (ED), *Girls are Powerful!: Young Women's Writings from 'Spare Rib'* (Sheba Feminist Publishers)
SHARPE, SUE, *Just Like a Girl! How Girls Learn to be Women* (Pelican)
THOMPSON, JANE, *All Right For Some! The Problem of Sexism* (Hutchinson)

Keith Waterhouse and his other writings

Keith Waterhouse is one of England's most widely known writers, as novelist, newspaper columnist, television and film script-writer. He was born in Leeds, in Yorkshire, in 1929, the fourth of four sons, and he went to the local 'Osmandthorpe Council School'. He started writing as a journalist in Leeds, and later moved to London, where he wrote for *Punch* and contributed a regular column to *The Daily Mirror* from 1970 until 1986, since when it has been appearing in *The Daily Mail*. He has received many national awards for his journalism, including the Granada Special Quarter Century Award in 1982. His novel *Billy Liar* is world famous not only in its original novel form but as stage-play, film, musical and a television series.

A complete list of his writings follows, but for wider reading by GCSE students we especially recommend the following. (Publishers are named in brackets.)

There is a Happy Land, a novel, edited by Alan O'Shea (Longman Imprint Books)
This is a humorous and very enjoyable account of a growing boy's everyday life in a northern town in the years before the last war.

Jubb, a novel (Michael Joseph)

Billy Liar, the play, by Keith Waterhouse and Willis Hall, edited by Michael Marland (Blackie Student Drama Series).
This is shorter than the novel and concentrates on his family.

Celebration: The Wedding and The Funeral, two short plays by Keith Waterhouse and Willis Hall (Michael Joseph and Evans Plays)

Screenplays

(with Willis Hall) include:
Whistle Down the Wind 1961
The Valiant 1962
Billy Liar 1963
A Kind of Loving 1963
West Eleven 1963
Man in the Middle 1964
Pretty Polly 1967
Lock up your Daughters 1969

TV films

Happy Moorings (with Willis Hall) 1963
How Many Angels (with Willis Hall) 1964
There is a Happy Land (from his own novel) 1965
The Warmonger 1970
Charlie Muffin (from novel by Brian Freemantle) 1979
This Office Life (from his own novel *Office Life*) 1984
The Great Paperchase (from the book *Slip up* by Anthony Delano) 1986

TV Series

The Upchat Line 1977
The Upchat Connection 1978
West End Tales 1981
The Happy Apple (from play by Jack Pulman) 1983
Charters and Caldicott 1984
Andy Capp 1988

(with Willis Hall):
Queenie's Castle 1970
Budgie 1971/72
The Upper Crusts 1973
Billy Liar 1973/1974
Worzel Gummidge 1979/87

Radio Plays

The Town That Wouldn't Vote 1951
There is a Happy Land 1962
The Woollen Bank Forgeries 1964

The Last Phone-In 1976
The Big Broadcast of 1922 1979.

Plays

Billy Liar, with Willis Hall, adaptation of the novel by Waterhouse (Michael Joseph and Blackie)
Celebration with Willis Hall (Blackie and Michael Joseph)
England, our England, with Willis Hall (Evans)
Squat Betty, and The Sponge Room, with Willis Hall (Evans)
All Things Bright and Beautiful, with Willis Hall (Michael Joseph)
Come Laughing Home, with Willis Hall (Evans)
Say Who You Are, with Willis Hall (Evans)
Whoops-a-Daisy, with Willis Hall (French)
Children's Day, with Willis Hall (French)
Who's Who, with Willis Hall (French)
Saturday, Sunday, Monday, (adapted from de Filippo) with Willis Hall (Heinemann)
The Card, (musical of Arnold Bennett novel) with Willis Hall
Filumena, (adapted from de Filippo) with Willis Hall (Heinemann)
Worzel Gummidge, (for children) with Willis Hall (French)
Mr and Mrs Nobody

Novels

There is a Happy Land
Billy Liar
Jubb
The Bucket Shop
Billy Liar on the Moon
Office Life
Maggie Muggins
In the Mood
Thinks
Our Song

General

The Passing of the Third Floor Buck
Mondays, Thursdays
Rhubarb, Rhubarb

KEITH WATERHOUSE AND HIS OTHER WRITINGS

Newspaper Style
Fanny Peculiar
Mrs Pooter's Diary
Waterhouse at Large
The Collected Letters of a Nobody
The Theory and Practice of Lunch
Wishful Thinking
The Theory and Practice of Travel

Longman Group UK Limited,
Longman House, Burnt Mill, Harlow,
Essex CM20 2JE, England
and Associated Companies throughout the world.

This edition first published 1989

Set in 10/11 point Baskerville, Linotron 202
Produced by Longman Group (FE) Ltd
Printed in Hong Kong

ISBN 0 582 01462 X

Acknowledgements

We are grateful to the following for permission to reproduce copyright material:

Angela Martin, from *You Worry Me Tracey You Really Do,* The Womens Press, page 163. Photograph by Christopher Barker, from *Portraits of Poets,* Carcanet Press page 182.

We are also grateful to the following for permission to reproduce copyright material:

Bloodaxe Books Ltd for poem 'Some People's Dreams pay all of their Bills' from *No, I'm Not Afraid* by Irina Ratushinskaya (1947), translated by David Mc Duff (Bloodaxe Books 1986); Chatto & Windus/The Hogarth Press on behalf of Mrs. Laura Huxley for extracts from *A Brave New World* by Aldous Huxley; Faber & Faber Ltd for poems 'As I Walked out one Evening' from *Collected Poems* by W.H. Auden & 'Engineers' Corner' from *Making Cocoa for Kingsley Amis* by Wendy Cope; Hamish Hamilton Ltd for an extract from *Summer of my German Soldier* by Bette Greene; Authors' Agents for poems 'Harlem, 'Little Old Letter', 'Final Curve', 'Still Here' by Langston Hughes from *Selected Poems* pubd. Vintage Books; the Author, Karl Mbeki for his poem 'Grandad' by Manelisi; John Murray Ltd for poem 'The Last Laugh' by John Betjeman from *Collected Poems*; Tuba Press on behalf of the Author, Paul Potts for his poem 'Note' from *Instead of a Sonnet* © Paul Potts 1944; the Author, Sista Rootz for her poem 'Their Plan'; Virago Press for poem 'Praise song for my Mother' from *The Fat Black Woman's Poems* by Grace Nichols. Copyright © Grace Nichols 1984; the Author, Mbeke Waseme (formally Sharon Bell) for her poems 'Walk Away', 'The Man', 'Joanne', 'Remember Me?' from *Exploring all of Me* (Peckham Publishing Project); Authors' Agents for behalf of The Literary Executors of the Estate of H.G. Wells for an extract from *The History of Mr Polly* by H.G. Wells; The Women's Press Ltd on behalf of the Authors, for poems 'The Miracle' by Maureen Hawkins, 'Don't Call me Mama' by Carole Stewart & '25.40pm (past morning)' by a-dZiko Simba from *Watchers and Seekers.*

We have unfortunately been unable to trace the copyright holder of the poem 'Goodbye' by Alun Lewis from *The Goodbye Book* by Ramsey & Toye pubd. Paddington Press 1979 and would appreciate any information that would enable us to do so.